CULTURALLY PROFICIENT INSTRUCTION

To Barbara Latimer Brown

who said to give something back to the community

CULTURALLY PROFICIENT INSTRUCTION
A Guide for People Who Teach

Kikanza Nuri Robins · Randall B. Lindsey
Delores B. Lindsey · Raymond D. Terrell

CORWIN PRESS, INC.
A Sage Publications Company
Thousand Oaks, California

For information:

Corwin Press, Inc.
A Sage Publications Company
2455 Teller Road
Thousand Oaks, California 91320
E-mail: order@corwinpress.com

Sage Publications Ltd.
6 Bonhill Street
London EC2A 4PU
United Kingdom

Sage Publications India Pvt. Ltd.
M-32 Market
Greater Kailash I
New Delhi 110 048 India

Printed in the United States of America

Library of Congress Cataloging-in-Publication Data
Culturally proficient instruction: A guide for people who teach / by
Kikanza Nuri Robins . . . [et al.].
    p. cm.
    Includes bibliographical references.
    ISBN 0-7619-7791-0 (c) —ISBN 0-7619-7792-9 (p)
    1. Multicultural States. 2. States.
I. Nuri Robins, Kikanza.
    LC1099.3 .C845 2002   2001003358

This book is printed on acid-free paper.

02   03   04   05   06   07   7   6   5   4   3   2   1

Acquiring Editor: Rachel Livsey
Editorial Assistant: Phyllis Cappello
Production Editor: Diane S. Foster
Editorial Assistant: Kathryn Journey
Typesetter/Designer: Larry Bramble
Indexer: Jeanne R. Busemeyer
Cover Designer: Michelle Lee
Cover Photo: www.comstock.com

Contents

Praise for *Culturally Proficient Instruction: A Guide for People Who Teach*

Culturally Proficient Instruction makes a unique contribution to the field of human relations training and equity-based education. In addition to being serious, thoughtful, and provocative, this new work is very user friendly and practical.

Stephanie Graham
Consultant, School Equity and Student Achievement
Los Angeles County Office of Education

A must read book for educators at all levels! *Culturally Proficient Instruction* provides invaluable information and self-reflective interactive exercises for BOTH the private and public sectors in which teaching is part of EVERYONE's job description.

Kaycee Hale
Executive Director, Research Centers of the Fashion
Institute of Design and Merchandising

I wish I'd had this helpful, practical book when I became a trainer and facilitator some 15 years ago. It would have saved me a lot of time, energy, and frustration! *Culturally Proficient Instruction* should be an essential text in every trainer's library today.

B. J. Gallagher Hateley,
Co-author of *A Peacock in the Land of Penguins:
A Tale of Diversity and Discovery*

Excellent materials written in layman's terminology. As a cultural competency educator, I am ecstatic to finally have a tool to help my organization to become culturally proficient.

Angeline McGill King
Core Values Coordinator
UCSD Healthcare

Culturally Proficient Instruction provides teachers and trainers everywhere with inspiring as well as practical tools to help their students as well as themselves.

Doug Kruschke
President, InSynergy

Culturally Proficient Instruction can help us train ourselves, our schools, our corporations, and our country to work with our diversity rather than against it. And it doesn't just tell us to, it tells us how.

Franz Metcalf, PhD
Author of *What Would Buddha Do?* and
What Would Buddha Do at Work?

Culturally Proficient Instruction is a book for all of us who have ever wondered what it would take to make school a place where *all* students flourish. A must-read for all who wish to harness the power of difference.

Patricia Martinez-Miller, PhD
Director of Faculty, School Management Program
University of California, Los Angeles

This book elicits discussions, descriptions, questioning, and responses that enable educators to move out of cultural destructiveness.

Sharon Rogers, PhD
Faculty Associate
Claremont Graduate School

The Cultural Proficiency team provides yet another important tool for instructors. The vignettes enable us to "walk with" others on this lonely and bumpy road to proficiency, while the reflections, prompts, and activities invite us to "go deeper" in self-examination.

Glenn E. Singleton
President, Pacific Education Group

The poignant stories in this book will seep into the critical consciousness of readers and guide them to transform their teaching practices to be culturally proficient.

Susan Taira, PhD
Co-Dean, The Fielding Institute

Culturally Proficient Instruction has been invaluable in guiding my practice as a management consultant, trainer, mediator, and business owner. The principles, strategies, vignettes, and reflections are practical, accessible, and thought-provoking. This book is a rare find.

Adena S. Wright, MBA
President, Wrightway Consulting

Foreword

Those whose professional calling involves shaping the lives of children stand at an interesting precipice, one in which the national conversation on reversing low performance in schools, decreasing the achievement gap, and ensuring that no child is left behind forms a new and challenging vista. This book both accepts the challenge and brings clarity and direction to the task. Its significance is not only that it orients us to a new literacy, but it also begins to answer the call for specific strategies for teaching all children. *Culturally Proficient Instruction: A Guide for People Who Teach* enables educators to act on the proposition that all children can learn and suggests knowable ways by which to achieve the goal.

The authors have gone to a great length to provide a set of conversations at ground-zero level. These conversations are instructive, rich, and reality based. At each turn of the page, the book mirrors tensions similar to those in public schools across America where demographic shifts have resulted in increasing numbers of children on playgrounds and in classrooms whose first language is not English; who are poor, African American, or Latino; or who exist in an underserved population. The strategies are not canned products. Rather, they derive from the constancy of dialogue between and among teachers and administrators whose courage and appetite for understanding the relationship between learning and culture compels them to think differently about teaching. This book gives a context and voice to the notion that culturally proficient instructors add value and dignity to children's lives and a dimension of professionalism to their artistry as teachers and leaders.

Reshaping the culture of the institution is a focus where the authors are equally generous in thought. Here, they shed light on the complex transformation of teachers, leaders, and ultimately, the culture of schools. In so doing, an inherent challenge is issued to the reader to think differently about how culture is the stage on which teaching and learning is performed. Culturally proficient language and behaviors of teachers produce a context of human caring, high expectations, and a diversity of instructional methods by which to teach all children. Such behaviors go far beyond the notion that teaching is solely about content and discipline. Indeed, this book is about relationships. It is about ways in which cultural proficiency is a bridge to cognition—an unrehearsed powerful set of lines between educators and their richly diverse audience of students. In *Culturally Proficient Instruction: A Guide for People Who Teach,* the story line holds true through the vignettes, the research, and the new practice. That is to say, culturally proficient instruction is a skill requisite for leaving no child behind. It is a core assumption, a habit of thought, a natural strategy in the repertoire of teachers and leaders working to educate all children. This book offers insight into the world of privilege in a world of despair and what can be done to close or eliminate the gap.

Educational research has for many years attempted to explain the relationship between teaching and learning and leadership and learning. The real question is, toward what end? My sense is that this book sheds some light on other domains where adequacy and proficiency will be needed for a new social order. These domains go far beyond academic work and test taking. In fact, the book suggests that culturally proficient instruction is a form of professional literacy for all educators. I applaud this work enthusiastically. It helps all of us to climb out of the doldrums over how difficult it is to educate all children to a 21st-century standard of living and knowing. It raises professional development, teaching, training, and leadership support to a new level of importance. It is hopeful. It avoids hand-wringing while providing pathways to a more culturally literate learning community. Perhaps most important, this book punctuates the need for conversations about race, class, and gender and the enormous implications that such conversations have on how we teach, who we teach, and toward what end.

Ron Edmonds created a new moral standard for schools by proclaiming, "All children can learn." He left it to others to reengineer school systems, to rethink classroom teaching strategies, professional preparation, behaviors, and attitudes of the adults to turn this notion into reality. *Culturally Proficient Instruction: A Guide for People Who Teach* pushes us up this moral hill, leaving behind no one whose courage, belief in children, and skill are brought into the classroom every day.

—Rudolph F. Crew, EdD

Introduction

Fifteen years ago, when we read Terry Cross's monograph, *A Culturally Competent System of Care*, we knew we had found something special. Since then, we have taken his work—the essential elements, the guiding principles, and the continuum—and applied them to a variety of organizations and industries. We have worked in hospitals, K through 12 schools, universities, not-for-profit organizations, and private businesses, introducing the basics of cultural competence and inviting the participants in our workshops to aspire to cultural proficiency. *Cultural proficiency* is a way of being that enables you to interact effectively in environments with people who differ from you. To be culturally proficient doesn't mean that you know everything there is to know about others. It means that you have the self-awareness to recognize how you—because of your ethnicity, your culture, and your life experiences—may offend or otherwise affect others. It means that you recognize how your ethnicity, your culture, and your life experiences may affect what you offer to others. It means that you have the skills to take advantage of *teachable moments* to tell about yourself and to learn about those who differ from you.

In our first book, *Cultural Proficiency: A Manual for School Leaders* (Lindsey, Nuri Robins, & Terrell, 1999), we addressed educational leaders, suggesting that they could make significant changes in their schools and communities by integrating cultural proficiency into their core organizational values. In this book, we have expanded our audience. This book invites you to reflect on your practice and craft as an instructor and to critically examine not only what you do but also the attitudes you bring to your work. We offer this book as your companion as you journey inward, discovering who you are and how you might create a community of culturally proficient practice in your classroom and among your colleagues.

Chapter 1 is the invitation; we ask you to remember a time when you realized that even with all your education and training, you didn't know enough to do your very best as an instructor. We invite you to reflect on why you chose to become a teacher, a professor, or a corporate trainer. We know that you may not have consciously made that decision when you were 20 years old, but we can surmise that if you are reading this book, you have made the decision to remain in the field. We don't tell you how to teach; we tell you how to build the relationships and create the environment so that everyone you teach can learn. Chapter 2 is a case story, which presents people like you and us, who aspire to improve their craft and be better instructors.

We define cultural proficiency in Chapter 3; talk about the barriers to cultural proficiency—a sense of entitlement and the unawareness of the need to adapt—in Chapter 4; and discuss the cultural proficiency continuum in Chapter 5. In each of the next five chapters, we discuss one of the essential elements of cultural proficiency: assessing culture, valuing diversity, managing the dynamics of difference, adapting to diversity, and institutionalizing cultural knowledge.

The final chapter is a call to action. After critically reflecting on your craft, we sincerely hope that you are inspired to do something a little differently or to continue doing what you are doing well with greater confidence. To help you reach that frame of mind, each chapter begins with questions that will help you focus on the topic to be addressed. Then, throughout the text, we ask you to stop reading to engage in activities, alone and with your colleagues, or to reflect on what you have read. Each chapter ends with an activity or a final set of questions that will take you more deeply into the topic. As you turn the pages of this book, you will find lots of space for writing. You become another author of the text as you write your responses to the questions and record your ideas for further work and reflection.

No good work is done in a vacuum. We would like to thank everyone who has helped us. Teachers, trainers, and professors who are members of our communities of practice have tried out our ideas, inspired new ones, and shared their own perspectives with us. Students, learners, and participants in our workshops have challenged us, encouraged us, and appreciated what we are trying to do. All of the people with whom we work and live have been a source of support and inspiration for the characters in the case story and for the values that inform our writing, our work, and our lives. Thank you.

Once again, Corwin Press has taken good care of us. Thanks, Gracia Alkema, for taking a chance on our ideas. Thanks, Rachel Livsey, for listening and listening and listening. Thanks, Phyllis Cappello, for your responsiveness and your hospitality. Shari Dorantes Hatch, you have a heart of gold and a golden touch. We cannot imagine having anyone else as our editor. Thank you so very, very much.

It is a rare and precious gift to do work that honors your passions, while working with people you love. This book is a tribute to decades of laughing and sharing and caring for one another as we tried to make a difference on the planet. It is the product of our friendship and collegiality. It is our gift to you, our reader.

—Kikanza Nuri Robins, Los Angeles, CA
—Randall B. Lindsey, Orange, CA
—Delores B. Lindsey, Orange, CA
—Raymond D. Terrell, Hamilton, OH

About the Authors

Kikanza Nuri Robins, MDiv, EdD, is an Organizational Development Consultant and a Certified Spiritual Director. She facilitates groups as they wrestle with and reconcile their conflicts, coaches managers as they make the internal shift to become leaders, and works as a change agent as people and organizations transform themselves from the inside out. Her experience includes work as an elementary school teacher, a university professor, a corporate trainer, and a pastor. She lives in Los Angeles, where she is the caregiver of two Chartreux cats—Manifest Justice and Munificent Concordance. (knurirobins@earthlink.net)

Randall B. Lindsey, PhD, is Professor Emeritus, California State University, Los Angeles. He has an educational consulting practice centered on issues related to diversity and has been a teacher, an administrator, and the executive director of a nonprofit corporation. He served for 17 years at California State University, Los Angeles, in the Division of Administration and Counseling. All his experiences have been with diverse populations; his expertise is in the behavior of white people in multicultural settings. It is his belief and experience that too often, white people observe multicultural issues rather than becoming personally involved with them. To that end, he designs—and implements with colleagues—programs that address the roles of all sectors of the society. (randallblindsey@aol.com)

Delores B. Lindsey, PhD, is Executive Director of the School Leadership Center at the Orange County Department of Education, Orange, California, where she leads and coaches teams and organizations using strategic visioning, team development, and leadership capacity building. She believes that the culture of an organization or team is best reflected by the language and stories used within the organization. She captures many of these stories in her writing and speaking. Drawing from her southern heritage, she shares her personal stories as a student, class-room teacher, middle-school principal, mother of two, and now, as a grandmother. Audiences and workshop participants appreciate her re-freshing look at life within an organization, as reflected in the stories and language of its members. (dblindsey@aol.com)

Raymond D. Terrell, EdD, is Distinguished Professor in Residence in the Department of Educational Leadership at Miami University in Oxford, Ohio. He previously served as an elementary school principal in Hamil-ton, Ohio, after retiring as a professor of educational administration and Dean of the School of Education, California State University, Los Angeles. He began his career as a public school teacher and administrator and has over 30 years of professional experience with diversity and equity issues. (terrelr@muohio.edu)

LET US HEAR FROM YOU

We would like to know what you thought about this book. We would also like to hear about your successes, your challenges, and the activities that you develop with the materials in the book. Please, let us hear from you.

The Cultural Proficiency Group
8306 Wilshire Blvd. #7019
Beverly Hills, CA 90211
Fax: (323) 939-8090

Part I

Laying the Foundation

1

Invitation

*To be a great teacher,
you must always be willing to learn.*

Getting Centered

Can you remember a time when you realized that even with your education and training, you didn't know enough? Can you remember the last time you asked yourself, "Why didn't anyone ever tell me about this?" Have you ever looked across a classroom of learners and wondered to yourself whether you had what you needed to reach each of them? Use this space for your answer.

_____

_____

_____

_____

_____

_____

This book is for people who teach. You may be an instructor in a K through 12 classroom, a university, or a corporate training room; you may call yourself a professor, a trainer, or an instructor. Whatever your teaching context or your title, when presenting subject matter to your students, three factors crucially affect your instruction: (1) your understanding of who you are and what you think about yourself, (2) your understanding of who the learners are and what you think about them, and (3) the way in which the learners receive you and the subject matter you are presenting.

⤙

With this book, we invite you to reflect on how you influence what goes on in your classroom and how you engage with your colleagues as a community of learners. We invite you to reflect on your practice as an instructor. We assume that you have mastered your subject matter, and we offer you an opportunity to reflect on how you teach, how you create an environment for learning in your classroom, and how the learners in your classroom respond to you and to one another.

⤙

Teaching in the United States is a cross-cultural encounter, involving a multiplicity of ethnicities, worldviews, lifestyles, and learning styles. Given these complexities, instructors need to examine how they address issues of diversity and to develop strategies that will increase their effectiveness. The strategy we offer in this book is cultural proficiency, which gives both instructors and learners the skills they need to learn how to work effectively with people who differ from them. *Cultural proficiency* is the *policies and practices* of an organization or the *values and behaviors* of an individual that enable that agency or person to interact effectively in a diverse environment. Cultural proficiency reflects the way an organization treats its employees, its clients, and its community.

⤙

This book is not for everyone who teaches. This book is for those of you who want to reflect on how you practice your teaching craft. After reading this book and engaging in the activities we describe, you will have examined some of your basic assumptions about your craft, and perhaps, you will have committed yourself to culturally proficient instruction. This commitment calls on you to change yourself, as well as to influence change in the institutions where you practice. The call to cultural proficiency invites individuals and institutions to better serve the learners who enter their classrooms.

Reflection

Are you aware of educational policies, practices, and procedures that demean individual learners or groups of learners? Do you have colleagues who either knowingly or unintentionally engage in practices that demean learners? Do you ever call these practices into question? Are you willing to confront either systems or individuals that dishonor your craft? Would you like to engage with colleagues in a process that will increase your awareness of diversity issues and your skills in addressing them? Write your responses here.

_____

_____

_____

_____

_____

_____

_____

_____

_____

_____

_____

_____

What Difference Does It Make?

Many adults can still recall and recite in order their elementary school teachers or the teachers who most influenced their lives. Successful physicians, attorneys, scientists, writers, and artists often acknowledge instructors as important role models for them. Despite this anecdotal evidence, for many years we had little or no research to support the hypothesis that teachers and teaching make a difference in learner achievement.

Since the mid-1990s, researchers have documented that high-quality instruction influences the success of learners. The factor that correlates most highly with learner success is instructor qualification, including teacher education, experience, and expertise (Darling-Hammond & Ball, 1997). Parker Palmer (1998) has described this expertise as a "capacity for connectedness" (p. 11). He states that good instructors are able to weave a complex web of connections between themselves, their subject matter, and their students. Culturally proficient instructors express this high value for connectedness.

Culturally proficient instruction is a way of teaching in which instructors engage in practices that provide equitable outcomes for all learners. Although individual instructors can offer culturally proficient instruction wherever they may teach, they most ably and effectively do so within culturally proficient organizations. A *culturally proficient organization* provides and supports conditions that create continuous learning opportunities for its members.

In Susan Rosenholtz's (1991) study, she found that instructors revealed two strongly held reasons for their continuous learning: (1) To deal sensitively with different learners, situations, and settings, instructors need a variety of skills and strategies, and (2) instructors need to modify their methodology to match changing needs of the learners. The research of Linda Darling-Hammond and Deborah Ball (1997), Kati Haycock (1998), and Susan Rosenholtz (1991) has clear implications for culturally proficient instruction. Through culturally proficient instruction, instructors inquire about best practices and reflect on their behavior in response to the various needs of learners rather than simply repeating rote skills and preparing for tests.

Learner success depends on the quality of instruction, regardless of other variables that influence achievement. High-quality teaching relies on an environment that fosters the ongoing learning of the instructor. To guide you in creating an environment fostering culturally proficient instruction, we have designed a hypothetical case, drawn from our own experiences with instructors in a variety of settings. This case introduces you to culturally proficient instruction, as it is developed and practiced within a community of instructors and learners. Throughout this book, various vignettes from the case illustrate aspects of culturally proficient instruction. Here is an example:

A few members of the Pine Hills High School accreditation team were curious about a phenomenon they discovered at the school. Some of the students, who otherwise were under-performing at this particular school, were performing at high levels in mathematics. The research team wanted to know what educational experiences these particular African American males had in common.

In time, they found that each of the young men had taken ninth-grade math with the same teacher, Ms. Brown. The research team was excited to interview Ms. Brown to learn more about the instructional strategies, the textbook, or the assessment strategies that she used to make this significant difference in the performance of her students. Ms. Brown was as surprised as the research team about these findings. When asked, "What do you do that is so different from what other teachers do?" she took only a few minutes to phrase her response: "I don't know what all the fuss is about. I teach the way I teach because I love each of them. Each child is special to me. *Why would I not teach each one?*"

good story)

We do not ask you to love each and every learner in your classroom. We do, however, suggest that you care about each and every learner. Furthermore, we believe that because you have chosen to teach and because you are seeking to be a culturally proficient instructor, you have already shown that you care. You care about what you teach, how you teach, and those you teach. By addressing the issues created by the diversity of your students, you are communicating to each learner that you care.

What Difference Do You Make?

You probably already believe that you can make a difference with your students because you have personally experienced the way in which some instructors have made a difference in your life. Take a moment to think now about the instructors who have most influenced you. Before you read more about culturally proficient instruction, reflect on how these influential instructors taught, and then consider their teaching practices.

⟞

Reflection

After thinking about the best instructors you have had, list the teaching practices they employed. What did they do? What happened in their class-rooms? Did they make you feel special? How? Can you remember whether they reached out only to you, or did they do something so that each learner felt special?

⟞

Perhaps your list included these elements: The instructors had mastered their subject matter and the craft of teaching, and they knew what they were doing. They cared that people learned. They created a space where it was safe to take the risks necessary for learning. They absolutely, unabashedly, loved what they were doing. They acknowledged the worldview of the learners and attempted to connect the learning experience to the context of the learner. These traits are commonly cited in conversations about influential teachers (Lindsey, 2000).

Karen Kent (1999) describes a series of stages of teacher develop-ment that she has observed. In her scheme, the two most advanced levels are the *experienced instructor,* who functions as a colleague, and the *accom-plished instructor,* who functions as a professional. The experienced instructor asks "What do my colleagues and I need to learn more about in order to improve our students' learning and performance?" (p. 16). The accomplished professional instructor asks questions such as, "How does good teaching practice get infused into educational policy and influence those policies that affect the quality of teaching and learning in the classroom?" (p. 17).

Experienced instructors want to know how culture has shaped them and their students. Professional instructors seek to take this cultural knowledge and institutionalize it into new policies and practices. These new policies and practices often replace ones that had limited students' access to knowledge and success in classrooms and training rooms. Thus, culturally proficient instructors seek to learn not only about the students but also about themselves in a cultural context. They also seek to create an environment in which learners are invited to explore the cultural contexts for who they are and how they relate to one another.

Culturally proficient instruction is an approach to teaching that invites the instructor to be more fully aware of the content of the instructional material and the context of the instructional practice. A culturally proficient instructor seeks to recognize what the learners bring to the instructional context and to acknowledge those contributions and perspectives in two ways: how the instructional material is delivered and how the instructor engages with the learners. Recall your own experiences as a learner. Think of a time when you felt that the teacher understood who you were and presented the information in a way that acknowledged you. Compare this with a time when you felt virtually invisible in the classroom.

As with most things in life, interpersonal relationships are essential to successful instruction. The process of teaching and learning is most effective when a relationship of trust and caring has been established. In our teaching, we seek to create environments in which the learners feel safe enough to take the risks they must take in order to learn. We can do so most easily through effective communication. If we are able to communicate that we understand the learner, we have laid the foundation for a trusting relationship.

Culturally proficient teaching and learning focus on communication and relationships. The first level of relationship is for instructors to have a well-developed sense of their own culture. Once instructors have this level of self-knowledge, they are better able to move to establishing trust and developing rapport with their students. Within an environment of trust, instructors can authentically communicate with the learners. When instructors succeed in creating this environment, they have begun to understand the culture of the classroom and the school organization in which it is found.

To be a culturally proficient instructor, you need not know all there is to know about the learners and their histories, worldviews, and cultural practices. Rather, as a culturally proficient instructor, you will acknowledge your need to learn from the learners as much as your need to impart information to them. In this book, we will introduce you to culturally proficient approaches to instruction, and we will invite you to reflect on how you can use these techniques with your learners.

Why Become Culturally Proficient?

As a *culturally proficient instructor*, you will create an environment in which you and your students become a community of learners engaged in culturally proficient practice—assessing the diversity of the classroom and the individuals in it, valuing diversity, managing the dynamics of their differences, adapting to those differences, and institutionalizing new ways of interacting as you and they learn more about yourselves and about one another.

Instructors have the responsibility not only to master the content they deliver but also to consider how they deliver that content. In doing so, contemporary instructors must guide learners from increasingly diverse backgrounds toward both academic success and effective human relations. Despite this increasing diversity, most people in the United States still function in largely segregated milieus. Because of this paradox, many instructors feel uneasy when asked to address issues of diversity in their learning environments.

During a workshop, Steve, a European American teacher, asked, "How can I ever have a dialogue with a person of color? I am afraid that if I ask a question or initiate a conversation, I might say something offensive and either be embarrassed or put down."

Irena, the workshop's Cuban American leader, explained, "Just breaking the ice can become a daunting task. Knowing more about how you respond can help you get started. We don't know how to carry on dialogues about our differences. People are afraid to ask questions for fear of being identified as racist. Others are offended when a speaker demonstrates a lack of knowledge, awareness, or sensitivity to the values, behaviors, and different perspectives that one might bring to any situation. We are unable to capture the natural curiosity that most people have when it comes to exploring differences. Fear dictates that we stifle inquiry about persons who are different. The notion of stifling curiosity should wave a flag to any person who teaches. It should stir the very depths of our moral souls to want to help all learners whom we encounter to find ways to satisfy their curiosity."

Why is it critical to address the issues of diversity now? The civil rights movement of the 1950s and 1960s created an atmosphere in which African Americans, women, older Americans, Gay men, Lesbians, Latinos, Asians, Native Americans, and other groups began to assert their rights to be respected and protected. *Group identity* and *self-determination* were watchwords within these movements. As we have raised awareness of human differences, we still struggle with trying to determine how each of us can respond most appropriately to the differences between the people we encounter each day. No longer can instructors evade the authentic issues arising from diversity that learners encounter daily. Nonetheless, many instructors are still reluctant to take action, as the following dialogue illustrates.

> Gladys, a European American workshop participant, asked, "Aren't you concerned that if we keep pushing this diversity stuff, we will simply further divide people? What's wrong with the 'melting pot' concept? Why can't we make one America?"
>
> Irena replied, "We can't afford to wait. Our students will be left out of a global economy if we don't better prepare them for the world. The reality facing many people today is that the number of encounters with persons who are different from them will increase; therefore, the number of differences reflected in these encounters will increase. High levels of mobility, greater rates of diversity in the workplace, and continued expansion of global economies and marketplaces make it likely that you will have an up-close and personal encounter with people from a number of ethnic groups, cultures, religions, socioeconomic levels, and sexual orientations."

In our world today, change is swift, and people now come together in a variety of venues without the awareness or skills to cope with the differences that they encounter. As the complexion and complexity of the learning populations become increasingly diverse, the people who teach remain chiefly Eurocentric and middle-class in their perspectives. As this disparity continues to grow, so does the need to embed cultural proficiency as an integral element within programs that prepare instructors to teach.

Who Should Use Culturally Proficient Instruction?

Many instructors face heterogeneous classrooms and training rooms that offer distinctive opportunities for meaningful dialogue and interaction among diverse persons. In addition, even in apparently homogeneous classrooms, learners are living and working within an increasingly diverse nation. In either setting, culturally proficient instructors will find opportunities for addressing the issues arising from diversity. Also, just as instructors must gain cultural proficiency, they must also teach other learners to acquire a sense of their own cultural identities and of their own reactions to people who differ from them. The culturally proficient instructor can then help learners develop a wider range of appropriate responses to the issues arising from diversity.

Culturally proficient instruction can take place in a wide array of teaching and learning environments. For instance, it may occur within a traditional setting, such as a public or private school or college, but it may also be within a corporation, public service organization, or any other of a diverse array of settings in which people need to gain knowledge or skills for a variety of reasons. To underscore the relevance of culturally proficient instruction to these diverse settings, we use the term *instructor* rather than *teacher* to identify those who teach. By using this term throughout this book, we address not only those who teach in traditional classroom settings but also those who do so in the rich array of teaching and learning environments we find today.

We address this book to all readers who identify themselves as professional instructors. We assume that you have mastered your subject matter and have developed competent teaching skills and expertise. Furthermore, we believe that you have committed yourself to the profession of teaching. Sergiovanni (1994) has noted that

> when first thinking about professionalism, attention is drawn to issues of competence. Professionals are experts, and this expertise entitles them to be autonomous. . . . Society demands that professionals not only be skilled, but also that their skills be used for good intentions. The moral engine that frames the dimensions of professional virtue about which instructors must constantly reflect includes:
>
> - A commitment to practice in an exemplary way
> - A commitment to practice toward valued social ends
> - A commitment not only to one's own practice but to the practice itself

- A commitment to sharing knowledge and skills with other professionals
- A commitment to the ethic of caring (pp. 75-76)

This book is for professionals who teach in public school classrooms, in colleges and universities, or in corporate training rooms. You may be wondering how we could possibly write a book that would be useful to such a wide range of people. The common denominator is not the business or profession with which you identify; it is your commitment to your practice of instruction. Your job title may or may not indicate that you are a teacher, but if, in your work, you are responsible for imparting knowledge to others, then this book is for you.

We are delighted that you have chosen our book as a means for enhancing your professional development. In it, we offer you an opportunity to reflect on your professional teaching practice. You may call yourself a professor, a trainer, or an instructor—the label doesn't matter. In addition to knowing your subject matter, it is important that you understand (1) who you are and what you think about yourself, and (2) who the learners are and what you think about them. In this book, we invite you to reflect on how you influence what goes on in your classroom and how you engage with your colleagues as a community of learners.

As you read this book, we want you to reflect on the way you teach, the instructional environment you create, and the way that learners respond to you and to one another. Personal reflection is one step in the process that will lead you to becoming a culturally proficient instructor. As such, you will continue to learn more about yourself and about how you affect learners. You will also develop skills for creating a community of culturally proficient practice among your learners.

Hilda Hernandez (1999) writes, "It is increasingly important for political, social, educational and economic reasons to recognize that the United States is a culturally diverse society, and that teaching is a cross-cultural encounter" (p. 3). For the American educational establishment to begin adequately to approach teaching in this way, we need to examine how we address issues of diversity and how to develop comprehensive change strategies for our classrooms and workplaces. Our strategy for intervention is *cultural proficiency*, which provides both instructors and learners with skills to learn how to work effectively with people who differ from them.

Cultural proficiency relates both to the *policies and practices* of organizations and to the *values and behaviors* of individuals that enable them to interact effectively in a culturally diverse environment. Cultural proficiency reflects the way an organization treats its employees, its clients, and its community. The call to cultural proficiency invites individuals and institutions to better serve the learners who enter their classrooms.

Through reading this book and engaging in the activities we suggest, you will reflect on how you practice your craft by examining some of your basic assumptions about teaching. We hope that as a result, you will commit yourself to striving for culturally proficient instruction. In doing so, you will commit yourself not only to changing yourself and your professional practice but also to changing the institutions where you practice. We believe that all instructors must commit to changing the institutions where they practice so that those institutions can better serve learners.

By committing yourself to exemplary practice, you are committing yourself to ongoing processes of self-reflection and self-improvement. As a culturally proficient instructor, you will have achieved sufficient self-awareness to know that constant renewal and self-improvement are fundamental to your practice. You will also begin to impart culturally proficient language, strategies, and practices through exemplary behavior. In this context, exemplary behavior will involve considering these factors in your teaching practice: learners' attitudes and perceptions, and communities' prior history and experiences with the institution in which you teach.

Cultural proficiency is an inside-out approach to the issues arising from diversity. The process of change must begin and end within each of us and within each of our institutions. Much of what has been done in addressing multiculturalism or diversity issues has focused on examining the *others*. If the inquiry begins by dealing with the others, prejudices and negative feeling about the others may be reinforced, and negative stereotyping and social distance may increase.

Most people who teach probably received years of training in their subject matter and much less training—perhaps merely a workshop or a single class—in the classroom complexities arising from differences in culture, class, race, gender, sexual orientation, language, and physical ability. Nonetheless, professional educators are being offered ever-expanding opportunities to gain information and strategies to help them move toward culturally competent behavior. School populations are growing, and private companies are investing more resources in education and training programs. In addition, instructors in any of these settings can increase their effectiveness by choosing to move toward cultural proficiency as they practice their craft.

We begin with comments that might very well have come from a school district superintendent, addressing the faculty in the week before classes begin. These comments are similar to those heard in colleges and other organizations as they begin to face the issues arising from diversity:

Are we willing to challenge insensitive comments or practices during routine conversations? I heard a colleague say to an African American female in a university class, "You already have an edge since you were probably admitted because of affirmative action." Are we willing to develop strategies that cause our colleagues to reflect on their language and behavior about critical social issues? Can you confront such insensitivity so that you become instructive rather than simply challenging? There is a fine line here in assessing whether the behavior is an unintended or uninformed act, or is an intended, direct assault on individuals or groups of "others." Posing questions and making comments that stimulate reflection can be productive. Similarly, are we willing to directly challenge and express disapproval of intentional hate speech and action? In either instance, if we are unwilling to engage our peers about such comments and actions, we show a lack of awareness of how to act in a culturally proficient manner. It is our professional obligation to address not only our own issues related to culturally proficient language and strategies with learners but also the language and actions of our colleagues.

Reflection

What do you think of the speaker's comments? How might you have felt had you been in the audience? Do you belong to a community in which critical reflection on the professional practice of instruction is invited or valued? What does that critical reflection look like?

_____

_____

_____

_____

_____

The Format of This Book

One way in which we address the diversity of teaching and learning environments that our readers may experience is through the use of a case that reflects the experiences of individual instructors. The vignettes we use throughout this book are composites of authentic stories—ours and those of our clients and colleagues. We have chosen these stories because they reflect both the obstacles individual instructors have faced and the means by which they have triumphed through their own efforts.

Chapter 2 immerses you in the stories of individual instructors who live, teach, and learn in the fictitious town of Maple View. We hope that their stories will speak to your situation. We use these examples to develop the concepts presented in this book.

In Chapters 3 through 11, we define cultural proficiency in detail and present the essential elements of cultural proficiency as tools for personal reflection and professional action. This book is designed as a guidebook that you can use alone or with your colleagues. Take your time with the reflection questions, and try the activities as we present them. We hope that the cumulative experience of working through this book will increase your cultural competence and move you closer to cultural proficiency. We invite you to reflect on who you are as an instructor and what you bring to the craft of teaching. We invite you to reflect on how you may be perceived by the learners in your classroom. Finally, we invite you to engage with them—and us—on a journey toward cultural proficiency.

Going Deeper

Think back to when you made the decision to become a teacher, a professor, or a corporate trainer. Was there a moment when you asked yourself, "Can I really do this?" Have there been times when you considered not teaching? Why do you still choose to teach?

_____

_____

_____

_____

_____

_____

_____

What difference do you make in the lives of your students?

_____

_____

_____

_____

_____

_____

Why do you seek to become a culturally proficient instructor?

_____

_____

_____

_____

_____

_____

_____

NOTES

The Case

Who Needs
Culturally Proficient Instruction?

One measure of culturally proficient instruction is to evaluate the words we use to describe our learners and the communities they represent.

⎯⎯

Getting Centered

Have you ever finished a lesson and wondered what you had missed or puzzled over why you felt off balance? Have you ever unintentionally insulted or hurt one of the learners in your classroom? Have you ever felt that there was more to teaching than mastery of your subject matter?

_____

_____

_____

_____

_____

_____

⎯⎯

This chapter introduces the numerous instructors and learners you'll get to know as you read this book. Their stories serve as a convenient tool for you to explore how to use culturally proficient instruction in your own teaching practice. Each character and each story is drawn from numerous real-life instructors and their authentic stories. These instructors demonstrate an array of teaching styles and experiences as they face the day-to-day challenges and successes of the complex world of teaching and learning. The instructors we describe teach in a variety of settings—public and private, prestigious and notorious, from prekindergarten through postgraduate, and in boardrooms and classrooms, corporations and public service organizations, offices and training centers. These settings for instruction may differ, but the instructors' experiences are very similar. The stories they share apply to teaching in the broadest and deepest sense of the word. Take the time to assess each story in the case before reading further.

Throughout this text, we are inconsistent in our use of personal address, both in the case that follows and in the vignettes from the case. When, as narrators, we refer to people in the case, after introducing them, we refer to the characters by their first names. When the characters are engaging with one another, the forms of address reflect the context of the exchange. For example, some colleagues address one another by their first names. Other colleagues are more formal and use Ms., Mrs., Mr., or Dr., as appropriate. In some parts of the South and some communities of color, people with doctorates or people who are held in high esteem are always addressed by their titles. Also, when there is a generational age difference between the speakers, the younger person, even if that person has greater rank in the organization, may address the older person using a title. As you read the case, notice these differences, and note the contexts. Sometimes, the simple use of titles or first names makes a significant difference in how a message is received. If, as an instructor, you are not sure which form of address to use, we recommend that you ask the learners in your classroom how they prefer to be addressed.

NOTICING A PROBLEM

Sam Brewer took time for his second cup of coffee as he read the morning paper. He skimmed the local news to see whether the open house announcement for Pine Hills High School was included in the community news section. As the new technology director at the school, it was Sam's responsibility to contact the newspaper office and make sure the announcement included the names of local businesses that had contributed financial resources to the new technology lab at the school. The public was invited to see for the first time the newest technology center available to students of Maple View.

Sam turned the pages quickly as he savored the last of his morning coffee. On each page, Sam saw advertisements and articles hailing the city as a great place to live. As a five-year resident of Maple View, Sam knew that the city's reputation as a prosperous community was strongly supported by local business advertisements. The reputation was further enhanced in the Maple View section of the daily *Metropolitan Times*.

Sam stopped turning the pages and looked quizzically at the headline on the editorial page, "The East Side Secret." The editor of the *Times* was accusing Maple View's city council of keeping the East Side secret from its new citizens on the affluent West Side. Incredulously, Sam continued to read. Now he was focused on "Letters to the Editor." One citizen had written,

> I've been a resident of Maple View for 25 years. I lived on Avenue C for 23 of those years. Two years ago I bought a home in Pine Ridge. I still do my banking at Community National Bank and I still go to church on the East Side. It is all one city. We get along very well, thank you!

The letter was signed, "Our Town." Sam put his empty cup in the dishwasher and headed out the door, still pondering the concept of East Side, West Side, and wondering what the real story was.

The next morning Sam read two responses to the previous day's editorial. One letter spoke knowingly of the efforts by city officials to keep the East Side secret out of public conversation. The other letter defended the city's efforts to present a unified front on all public issues. Two days later, another letter appeared,

> Dear Editor,
> I won't sign my real name to this letter because I have to live here and work here with my neighbors in Maple View. But I want people to know that things are not what they seem here in our little city. I have lived on the East Side of town

since I was born. My parents don't talk much about how they are treated here because they are afraid they might lose their jobs at the produce factory. We are farmers and live in the farmers' housing project at the end of the Avenues. But I know. I see it and I feel it. My children and I are treated the same way that my parents have been treated over the years. People in the city are usually nice and polite, but we are never treated like we really belong here. Even our children are treated differently at school. My kids are put in special classes even before they have a chance to prove what they know. Our kids can read. Our homes aren't lit by candle-light, and we don't sing songs around a campfire. We read aloud to our children. We tell our family stories. We go to church. We pay our taxes. We work very hard. And we are the secret of the East Side.

The letter was signed, "Grapes of Wrath." Sam Brewer, a teacher at Pine Hills High School, the new high school on the West Side of the city, was putting the pieces together. Underneath the surface of a diverse and unified community image were real questions about equity. Was racism or bigotry or ignorance at work here? Were these questions being asked by well-meaning people who had the best interests of the community in mind? What did he really know about this community in which he had chosen to live and teach? To help him sort through his own thoughts, Sam decided to chronicle what he knew about Maple View.

GETTING TO KNOW MAPLE VIEW

Maple View is a small city located within a major metropolitan area. The city's population of 200,000 comprises mostly middle-income and working-class folks who live and work within the community. About 5% of Maple View residents are in the upper tax bracket and work in the top-paying management positions in the area's high-tech industries and corporations. About 30% of them are considered working poor and rely on government assistance for child care and health care for their

families. For the most part, families in this community, regardless
of income, send their children to the local public schools, shop at
the area businesses, bank at the local banks and credit unions,
seek health care at the community hospital and neighborhood
clinics, and attend local churches, temples, and synagogues.

The Internet has made many government services readily
available to many Maple View residents. According to a recent
newspaper survey, however, only 25% of Maple View residents
have access to the Internet in their homes. The survey also indicated that 90% of the homes having personal computers and
access to the Internet are located on the West Side of the city.

Area builders and the area's leading real estate business owners perceive Maple View as a prosperous community partly because
of the community's master plan development. However, the waiting list for low-rent public housing indicates a highly diverse economic environment. A major state highway divides the master-
planned, affluent West Side from the downtown and middle- and
low-income housing developments on the East Side. A large shop-
ping mall opened five years ago to serve the upscale master-
planned community. The downtown area on the East Side is
served by mom-and-pop merchants, including a locally owned
hardware store and a drugstore owned by the same family for three
generations. The East Side residents typically shop at the Wal-
Mart and Target stores on that side of town.

The large, 450-bed teaching hospital, University Medical Center (UMC) located at the north end of Maple View, serves the
health and medical needs of all Maple View residents. UMC has
served the community for more than 25 years. Two years ago, the
chief administrative officer at the hospital spearheaded the development of a community-wide leadership project, "Leadership
Maple View." The project invites community participants to apply
for a one-year term. Participants who are accepted for the project
agree to serve with their colleagues on leadership teams in which
they identify a specific community-based need and design a team
response to that need. Participants receive extensive leadership
training during their one year of service. The leadership projects
are supported by corporate and federal grant funds. Projects that
have been implemented by Maple View's leadership teams include
improvements to the city park located adjacent to the city hall,
construction of pedestrian walkways near the hospital and shop-
ping areas, and construction of two large billboards placed at the
entrances to the city. The city's leadership theme, "Growing Our

Own Leaders," was used as the focal point on the billboards: "Welcome to the City of Maple View: We Grow Leaders."

The hospital, community college, and school district employ professional staffs of instructors, human resource officers, and administrators, as well as food service, maintenance, and transportation personnel. In combination, these agencies employ the largest numbers of community residents.

A small, corporate farming area provides vegetables for a nearby packing company. Both companies employ more than 200 migrant workers for the seasonal crops. The migrant workers live in corporate housing near the East Side farming area of Maple View. The demand for migrant workers is growing as the current demand for produce increases. The second-generation migrant families continue to live in the East Side housing projects and to send their children to the same local school the parents had attended as children.

The economy of Maple View is prosperous, and the Chamber of Commerce calls it "a great place to live and work." *Parade* magazine recently listed it in the "200 Top Small Cities in the Nation to Work and Raise a Family." The school district is in the top 15% in the statewide testing program. The publicity and recognition that the city has received, combined with upper-level master-planned housing, middle-income housing, and outstanding employment opportunities have resulted in a projected annual population increase of 5%.

MAPLE VIEW SCHOOL DISTRICT

The ethnic diversity of the city's population is reflected in the student population in the local school district. Of the 25,000 students in the public schools, 35% are European Americans; 30% are Hispanics from Central America, South America, and the Caribbean; 20% are Asian Americans (1st- and 2nd-generation families from Korea and the Philippines, and 3rd- and 4th-generation families form China); 10% are African Americans; 3% are Native Americans; and 2% are Pacific Islanders. Twenty percent of the total student population is in special education programs, and 10% of the students are learning English as a second language. The district reports that seven different primary languages are spoken by its students.

The local school district responded to the increased student population in the West Side area by building the new Pine Hills Elementary School for Grades K through 5 and the new Pine View Middle School for students in Grades 6 through 8. One year ago, the district opened the new state-of-the-art Pine Hills High School on the West Side of the city. The old Maple View High School facility on the East Side of the city was converted to a community school for at-risk students, adult school students, and community recreation organizations. The school district maintains ownership of the property and has a joint-use partnership agreement with the city council. The downtown and East Side students continue to be served by the original Maple View Elementary School (Grades pre-K-5) and Maple View Middle School (Grades 6-8) in the district.

The local school board and the superintendent and other district office administrators have published a shared vision to serve all learners in the district with outstanding teachers, appropriate materials of instruction, and high standards for student performance. Board members are elected at large to serve the entire district rather than any particular geographical constituency. The current superintendent has served the district for the past 10 years and recently announced his retirement, effective at the end of the current school year. A community-wide retirement celebration is being planned by a committee comprising members from the city council, parks and recreation commission, chamber of commerce, and two members of the seven-member board of Maple View School District. The school board is currently involved in seeking a replacement for the retiring superintendent.

MAPLE VIEW INSTRUCTORS

Maple View School District employs 850 teachers, only a few of whom are described here. Nonetheless, their stories offer a representative sampling of the kinds of issues that teachers face and of the kinds of experiences, approaches, and attitudes these teachers bring to the teaching and learning environment.

■ Sam Brewer

Samuel "Sam" Brewer reviews his notes and description of Maple View. He then thinks about who he is and how he fits into this picture. Sam, a 34-year-old European American male, teaches computer science classes at Pine Hills High School. He is single and lives in one of the older, gentrified homes near downtown. Sam moved to Maple View five years ago and has been dating Suzie Cheng, a human relations specialist at Tri-Counties Community College (TCCC), for the past six months. Sam met Suzie on one of his visits to the college computer lab to talk about taking some of his students to the lab after school two afternoons a week.

Last year, Sam voluntarily transferred from Maple View Middle School because the high school principal believed that Sam's tech skills could be put to better use at the high school than at the middle school. One colleague at the high school even said to him, "Come on up to the high school, Sam. You know those kids on the East Side don't even have computers at home in the first place. They'll get what they need in the basic classes anyway. We need you for our advanced kids."

Sam agreed to the transfer only if he could be the new director and make decisions about the technology plan and budget. The high school principal agreed to Sam's request. Sam's transfer left Maple View Middle School without a computer teacher. Sam worried about the kids he'd left behind at the middle school and about what would happen to them without him to speak up for them when it came to the school district's technology plan. The new Pine View Middle School, located on the West Side, had been designated as the state-of-the-art middle school in the entire area, and Maple View had received a small state-funded technology grant for the East Side's middle school. Sam had written the grant application and was excited when the school was awarded the funds, but the money didn't go very far in purchasing the hardware needed just to get the school access to the Internet and a few new computers for the technology lab.

Sam is often troubled by the lack of equal funding given by the school district to the East Side schools. However, he is excited to be at the new high school and to have the opportunity to direct the overall technology program for kids there. He hopes to work something out with the director of technology at TCCC for the high school students from the East Side to have access to the college computer lab at least two nights a week and maybe even get some college credit for extra courses they take in the evenings.

Sam also realizes his new job will open additional opportunities for his own professional growth with the district. He has been asked to design the districtwide technology training for teachers over the summer. So far, however, very few teachers from the East Side schools have signed up for the training. Sam asked one of his friends, the assistant principal at Maple View Middle School, "Rose, why haven't more of your teachers signed up for tech training yet?"

"Are you kidding? Most teachers never get to use the tech lab. There are hardly enough computers for the writing classes to use anyway. I bring my own laptop from home so the kids can get on the Internet and find some science resources, but other than that, our kids never get computer time. So why waste my time getting trained, when I have nothing new to work with?"

Sam worries about his teacher friends, but most of all, he worries about the kids at Maple View Middle School. He wonders if this is this part of the "East Side secret." He decides that it is time to have a deeper conversation with his friend Rose.

■ Rose Diaz-Harris

Rose is 33 years old and until last year had been a sixth-grade teacher at Maple View Middle School. This year she is the assistant principal. She has been a school district employee for 13 years, first as a teacher's aide (for 5 years), then as a teacher in the district (for 8 years). She completed her master's degree 2 years ago.

Sam has known Rose for the past three years. They have had long conversations about teaching in the middle grades. They share concerns about equity (fairness) issues in education. Sam counts Rose among the top 10 instructors he knows. She was an outstanding teacher and is a great friend.

Rose is a fluent Spanish speaker and has taught both her children to speak Spanish, the language of their grandparents. Several times last year, Rose had invited Sam to her home to visit with her parents and family. Rose's parents are migrant workers and have lived in the farmers' housing project since they moved to Maple View from Central America, 30 years ago. Rose and her husband, James Harris, recently bought a new home on the affluent West Side.

James is the director of the Department of Human Resources and Staff Development at TCCC, which is located on the older, less affluent East Side of Maple View. The college was established in 1955 as part of the statewide master plan for higher education. Tuition, textbooks, and resident housing are offered to students at substantial savings, compared with the State University four-year program. TCCC received the "Achievement of Excellence" Award in 1999 for the program in multicultural staff development and employment practices, which James helped design and implement.

Rose and James have two children, Josh and Susan. Josh is in the sixth grade and attends Pine Hills Elementary School, located near their new home in Pine Ridge Acres. Although the school district would grant an attendance transfer for Josh to attend the school where Rose works, Rose and James decided to have Josh attend the neighborhood school because Josh's friends attend that school and they live within walking distance from the school. They decided, however, that Susan would attend the second grade at Maple View Elementary School, where she had attended kindergarten and first grade. Rose wanted Susan to be in Ms. Pearson's class because Rose had worked with Ms. Pearson recently on a districtwide special education project. Rose believes that Ms. Pearson truly understands Susan's learning disability and will help Susan be successful in the regular classroom. Rose also thinks about how to make learning opportunities equitable for special-needs students at Maple View Middle School.

■ Suzie Cheng

Another important person in Sam's life is Suzie Cheng. Suzie is the newly appointed human relations specialist at TCCC. Her supervisor is James Harris, husband of Rose Diaz-Harris. Suzie is a third-generation Chinese American. She recently moved to Maple View from the nearby metropolitan area, seeking a better job opportunity and affordable housing. Suzie is 29 years old, single, and enjoys sports and recreation. She also places high value on community involvement and enjoys being a member of the Maple View Recreation Committee. She is a member of Leadership Maple View, and during her one-year term, she hopes to initiate a project to improve the old park on Avenue A to create a youth development center for sports activities. Suzie hopes that by working with the teens on the East Side, she can encourage more students to attend the community college when they graduate from high school. Suzie hopes her new projects will help students have access to opportunities that their perceived deficits have denied them.

Suzie recently met Sam Brewer, who had been in and out of the college's tech center quite a bit, trying to set up a schedule for his students to use the college computer labs in the evening. Suzie was pleased to have finally met someone who had a similar education and community values. Suzie and Rose have also become good friends, and the two couples—Sam and Suzie and Rose and James—get together occasionally to ride bikes or go out for dinner. Suzie and James try not to discuss work, but Sam and Rose are always talking about their schools and their teaching experiences. Suzie and James explain to Sam and Rose that they teach, too. Suzie said to Rose recently, "You don't have to have children seated in desks, lined in rows, with books in their hands to be a teacher. My students are adults who have jobs and families, sit at round tables, and discuss their learning goals." She wasn't sure that Rose saw her point.

Suzie had been the orientation trainer for classified employees in the personnel office at the State University. In her new role at TCCC, she is responsible for designing and implementing a training program for department managers and administrators in the areas of conflict resolution, communication, and employee relations. Because Suzie's background is in cultural studies, she was hired to help the organization work through some of its issues of diversity in the workplace.

■ Helen Williams

Maple View School District has many outstanding employees, some of whom Sam had met at the Outstanding Teacher Awards Dinner last spring. He wondered now, if he interviewed them, what they might say about teaching and living in Maple View. He remembered meeting Helen Williams, who had lived and worked in the community for many years and was well thought of by other teachers in the district. Sam decided to visit with Helen in her classroom one afternoon after school.

Helen is an African American preschool teacher in her early 60s, who has been teaching preschool children in Maple View "all her life." When Sam asked her how long she had been teaching in the district, Helen responded, "I moved here with my family when I was only five years old. My father was the minister at the

First Methodist Church for 15 years before he retired and moved back to his home in Louisiana. My mother was the head librarian at Maple View Public Library until she died, two years before my dad's retirement."

Helen and her husband, Leonard, have lived in the same house on Avenue B for the past 42 years. Leonard is the day manager and dispatcher at MedSupplies.com. He transferred to the company after working 20 years at the parent company, Med Supplies and Equipment Co. in a nearby city. Helen was pleased that "the company treats Leonard well. He is one of their most loyal employees. The transfer was a promotion for him and a way to get him closer to home for his last five years with the company."

Helen has decided not to retire until she absolutely has to. "These preschool children have been my children," she said, "and I'm not leaving them anytime soon." From time to time, Helen and Leonard have taken in foster children as their way of parenting children who needed their love. Helen was honored as Maple View's 1995 Outstanding Citizen of the Year for her leadership in working with at-risk children in the community.

"Every morning of the school year for the past 42 years, I have walked the two blocks from my home on Avenue B to this classroom at Maple View Elementary School," Helen chronicled her story for Sam. For the past 20 years, not only has Helen taught her classes, but she has also coordinated the school's Head Start Program and English Language Learners Program. The principal at the school recently talked to Helen about some of the mandated changes in the programs at the school and requested that Helen go for some training at the district office to better understand some new opportunities for funding support for the preschool. Helen was excited that the principal asked her to go for the training because the younger teachers "just don't understand what these children need."

Sam asked Helen what she thought about the recent letters to the editor and the editorial about the so-called East Side secret. "What is so secret about it? The families on this side of town know what is happening. It is no secret over here. Go talk to some of the teachers over on the West Side and let them tell you how it looks from over there."

Sam decided to do just that.

■ Eduardo "Ed" Gonzalez

"Hi, Ed, remember me? I'm Sam Brewer. I called you earlier in the week. Have you got a minute to chat with me?" Sam asked Eduardo "Ed" Gonzalez, a teacher who served on the district technology committee.

"Sure, come on in," Ed responded to Sam's invitation. "My class just left, and I was going to grade a few papers, but that can wait. How have you been doing?"

Ed is in his early 40s. He is a widowed father of three school-age children. Ed's wife, Lupe, died two years ago from cancer. Lupe had taught second grade at Pine Hills Elementary School, and Ed had taught the third grade. Ed and Lupe had both transferred to the new school when it opened. Their classrooms were directly across the hall from each other. They both had taught at Maple View Elementary before transferring to Pine Hills.

After Lupe's death, Ed tried to remain at Pine Hills, but the memories were too painful for him. He requested a transfer back to Maple View Elementary School, where they needed an English Language Learner (ELL) teacher. Ed's parents had immigrated from Cuba, so Ed spoke Spanish fluently, but he had never taught an ELL class before. Pine Hills Elementary did not have ELL students, so there was not a need for the program there. Ed decided to take the transfer so that he would learn something new himself. His first year back at Maple View was harder than he had thought it would be. His students struggled with reading because they could not speak English. Ed decided it would be better to teach the students to read in Spanish than it would be to try to teach them English and try to teach them to read at the same time. He didn't feel he was very successful, but no one complained. He took a Spanish refresher course over the summer to help him improve his own use of the language.

He decided to take his three children for a two-week trip to Mexico to visit Lupe's relatives. He had never previously visited Mexico, even though Lupe's parents had told them of her relatives there. He hoped the visit would help with the grieving process, allow his children to get to know their extended family, and give him opportunities to practice his Spanish.

"How do you like being back here at Maple View Elementary School, Ed?" Sam was a little embarrassed about sounding so personal with his first question. "What I mean is, I know you taught over at Pine Hills for a few years and just wanted to get your perspective on the 'East Side, West Side' talk from the news-paper. You've seen it from both sides of town, so to speak."

"You've asked a really tough question, you know." Ed seemed hesitant at first. "I'm not sure I can shed much light on the sub-ject. The kids on the West Side just seem to have it easier than the kids over here. I mean those kids come to school with everything they need. Kids over here seem to be missing out—not missing school, just missing opportunities. They don't want charity. We don't need handouts for our kids. We need access to the best cur-riculum and materials and technology. We need opportunity. The kids have the potential. We hold the promise."

"Would you be willing to work with me on a community project that will help us to keep that promise, together?" Sam asked Ed, not even sure of what he was proposing.

"Count me in," Ed replied. He then asked a tough question of his own, "But where do we start?"

Sam and Ed decided to continue the work that Sam had started. They made a list of names of people in the community who would have information and experiences to help them piece together the East Side puzzle. Once they had made their list, Sam and Ed each took several names and started the interviews. After two weeks, Ed and Sam reviewed their findings with each other. Sam had started his interviews with one of his colleagues at the high school, Charlene Brennaman.

■ Charlene Brennaman

Charlene is the divorced mother of Brian, a ninth-grade stu-dent at Pine Hills High School. Brian's father, Bret, travels exten-sively as a sales representative for a large insurance firm. He lives out-of-state and visits Brian in the summer and again during Chanukah. Bret and Charlene divorced two years after the car accident that left Charlene confined to a wheelchair. At age 35, Charlene struggles to make ends meet on her teacher's salary because she can't always count on Brian's father to send support payments, especially if sales are slow. She also needs medical attention and physical therapy regularly. Just getting to her class-room each day is a challenge.

Brian is a computer genius and loves his classes at the new tech center at the high school. His favorite teacher is Sam Brewer. Brian can hardly wait for Sam to arrange time at the community college for Brian and the other students to take classes after school in the computer lab. Brian's old computer can't be upgraded anymore, and he wants to have access to the computer technology.

Charlene enjoys teaching at the new middle school. She is one of the eighth-grade math teachers. She designed a course, "Algebra for All," that allowed all eighth-grade students to take Algebra I. Charlene knows how much Brian wants to go to college. Prior to this course, only the honors students could take algebra in the eighth grade. Now, students like Brian, who did not qualify for the honors program, will not be a year behind the honors student classmates in the college-prep program.

Charlene had to work hard to convince the other math teachers that eighth graders could do well in algebra if effective teaching strategies were used. As she continues to work with the teachers, she realizes that several of them do not really believe that all their students can be successful. She also realizes that the teachers are not as skilled at teaching algebra as they were at teaching regular math. She thinks it is easier for teachers to blame the learners than it is to admit that they need more and different instructional strategies.

Charlene's principal asked her to chair the math department this year. She hopes to design another new course, seventh-grade pre-algebra. She has also contacted the chair of the math department at the State University to arrange an algebra-for-teachers course to be offered online for the math teachers at both middle-grade schools.

■ LuAnn Steiner

LuAnn is another person on Sam's list who had worked with him on a curriculum committee. In her mid-30s, LuAnn Steiner is European American and a closeted Lesbian. She lives with Julie, her "roommate." LuAnn and Julie are life partners but have chosen to keep their relationship secret from their families and friends. Julie is the administrative assistant to the president at Tri-Counties Community Hospital. LuAnn teaches sixth grade at Pine Hills Elementary School. They plan to live openly as a Lesbian couple when they move out of state in about five years.

LuAnn is an outstanding middle-grades teacher. She has received several awards for "Peace Weavers," the social justice curriculum that she designed. She serves the school district as a master teacher who mentors new teachers coming into the district. This year, Dr. Barbara Campbell, assistant superintendent for curriculum and staff development, wants LuAnn to work with her in examining all the instructional materials for racial and gender bias. LuAnn is not sure why Dr. Campbell wanted her on the committee, but she agreed to help if she could. She was even more surprised when Dr. Campbell asked her to chair the district's Committee for Culturally Proficient Instruction.

LuAnn spent her summer reading and trying to understand more about the concept of cultural proficiency. She hopes this work will help her to help her colleagues become more attentive to the needs of all learners in their classrooms. LuAnn recalls painfully some of her own childhood experiences in classrooms when her teachers turned away when other kids made fun of her, especially in Maple View Middle School. LuAnn vowed to create a classroom where each child would feel safe and respected. She has held true to that commitment over the years as a classroom teacher. Now she wants to help other teachers learn to do what she intuitively knew how to do. She thinks that maybe cultural proficiency is a way to reach and teach other teachers about creating conditions in which each child can enjoy success, *regardless* of how the child looks, dresses, or sounds—or maybe even *because* of how the child looks, dresses, or sounds. She wonders, though, why this concept is not being used outside of the public schools. Many college students attend her church and tell her of painful experiences caused by college instructors.

■ Barbara Campbell

At the top of Ed's list is a highly influential leader in the community and the school district, Dr. Barbara Campbell. After receiving her PhD six years ago, Barbara implored her colleagues to call her "Dr. Campbell" in front of the high school students. One teacher responded by saying, "Well, I guess you have to be a role model for the black kids, but you'll always be 'Miss Barbara' to me."

Dr. Barbara Jones Campbell is an African American in her mid-40s. She moved to Maple View as a high school English teacher. She completed her administrative training at State University during her tenth year as a teacher, after which she was quickly promoted to assistant principal at Pine Hills High School. Some members of the community and many faculty members at the high school felt that Barbara received her promotion as part of the district's affirmative action program. Barbara was aware of the perception that her colleagues had, and she had decided to prove herself by being an outstanding assistant principal. "Of course, it wouldn't take much," Barbara mused to herself, "to outperform the other assistant principal, Mr. Cooper." Fred Cooper had been the assistant principal at the high school for 15 years when Barbara joined the administrative staff. In charge of student suspensions and facility supervision, he had shown little initiative and knew very little about helping learners and instructors be more effective in the classrooms. He functioned more as an administrative assistant than he did as an educator. The staff viewed him as "our assistant principal," serving their needs first and students' needs last.

The current principal, Dr. Robert Hanford, told Barbara during her first meeting with him, "Now, young lady, you are going to show people around here that you are just as good as they are. Just like you have done all your life, you'll have to prove to some people that you are smarter than they think you are. I want to make sure that you are successful at this job. The first thing you need to do is enroll in a doctoral program. That'll show 'em. Nobody was surprised when I got my PhD. That was expected of me. But not you. No, they don't expect that you can do it. It is up to you to prove them wrong, so others who come after you won't have to overcome low, or no, expectations."

Robert continued, "Let's start by giving you Mr. Cooper's office. It is much larger and has nicer furniture in it. I'll move him to the office in the other building. He'll be fine with the move, I'm sure." Barbara spent her first year as assistant principal trying to repair the damage done by Robert's well-intended decision to move Fred Cooper's office and give Barbara the better office space. In contrast, the best thing Robert did for Barbara was to recommend her to the State University doctoral program. Four years later, after Robert retired, she became Dr. Campbell and the new principal. Fred Cooper was promoted to director of the Community School.

After five years as a high school principal, Barbara was promoted to the district office as assistant superintendent for curriculum and staff development. She has been highly successful in designing professional development that includes a focus on culturally proficient classrooms and schools. She created the district's Committee for Culturally Proficient Instruction. Teachers have responded to the training by requesting more workshops on how to teach all students while maintaining high academic standards. Her district office colleagues view Barbara as the probable next superintendent for the district. Barbara smiled, inside and out, when she recently overheard one of the young, European American teachers say, "I hope that someday I can be half the teacher Dr. Campbell is. She is my role model!"

■ Alicia and Alberto Alvarez

Ed had met a young couple at one of his children's sports events and decided to add them to his interview list. Alicia and Alberto are both in their early 40s and enjoy being the parents of three school-age children. Alberto is the assistant manager at MedSupplies.com. Alicia and Alberto are happy to participate in school activities with their children. Alicia was elected to serve on the School Site Council for Maple View Middle School. She also volunteered to serve as one of the parent chaperons for her son Bert's sixth-grade overnight camping trip to the local mountains. Alberto and the younger two children, Allie and Cee-Cee, joined them, so it became a family outing as well. Alberto's company, MedSupplies.com, donated the use of one of their delivery vans for the overnight school trip. Alberto stocked the van with food supplies and science equipment for the trip.

Alicia became aware of the outdoor science education program at her first School Site Council meeting for the year. When the principal said that not all students attended outdoor education, Alicia wanted to know, "Who doesn't, and why not?" One of the teachers said, "The farm kids don't go because their parents don't care whether they get to go or not. They just keep them at home to add extra workers in the fields while the other kids are studying hard at outdoor education. There's nothing we can do about it if the parents don't care, is there?"

In years past, students who could not afford the trip were assigned to the library for the three days the other sixth graders were on the science trip. The students who were left behind were assigned written projects about outdoor science. Most of the students who could not afford the trip lived in the farmers' housing project. The families were embarrassed to send the children to school because everyone would "know" why they were in the library for three days. So the parents would keep the children home and have them work in the fields those days to learn about the importance of rain for the crops, soil nutrients, and plants and animals living together. The children learned that good crops produced good incomes. When the children returned to school after their three days of absence, they were given F grades for unexcused absences. No one at the school even questioned why so many of the farm kids were absent at the same time.

Alberto and Alicia had chaired the fundraising activities for the school so that those students who couldn't afford the $150 for the trip could receive scholarships to cover their costs. This year, because of Alberto and Alicia's hard work and commitment, all the children in the sixth grade took the outdoor science trip.

Alicia is the director of Training and Staff Development at University Medical Center. She appreciates the flexible schedule that she has at work so that she can attend school activities with her children. Her job requires that she design and deliver, or contract out, all the nonmedical training at the hospital. Often, her supervisor, the vice president of Human Resources, tells Alicia what training topics she should offer. Alicia has suggested conducting a needs assessment to help determine what training the department should offer. Her supervisor refuses to use that approach, and in response to Alicia's most recent request to survey the staff, the vice president said, "Why create extra work for ourselves? We know what they need, so just put the stuff together and give it to them."

Alicia wonders what her next career move will be. She isn't sure how long she can continue to work for a supervisor who undermines her work and doesn't share her values regarding high-quality, meaningful professional development.

Stuart Montgomery

Sam knew that one person he would interview was the most vocal teacher in the district. Stu, as his friends call him, is a European American, 30-year veteran of Maple View School District. He and his wife, Beverly (who, like Stu, is in her late 50s), live in one of the new homes in Pine Ridge. They were among the first residents of the new community. Stu and Bev had lived downtown for many years in one of the old Victorian homes that Beverly had inherited from her great-grandfather, one of the founders of Maple View. Along with the house, Bev and Stu inherited a small fortune that ensured they would live quite well for the rest of their lives. Bev has always been active in the women's service clubs in Maple View. Stu has enjoyed their membership at the City Club, where he plays golf every weekend. He and Bev use the summer months, when Stu isn't teaching, to travel.

Stu teaches physical education at Pine View Middle School. He had enjoyed teaching PE until five years ago, when the state implemented a curriculum for physical education and fitness. Since then, Stu has spent most of his time resisting the new curriculum and continuing to teach the team sports that he has taught with success in years past. He transferred to the new middle school when it opened a few years ago. The Pine View Middle School parents really want the school to produce top-level sports teams. Therefore, Stu has convinced the school's administrators that he is teaching the kids the sports skills they need to be successful at the high school. Two new experienced PE teachers, from neighboring school districts, were hired last year because of the increase in student enrollment. They moved to Maple View to take advantage of the low-cost, new homeowner loans offered to teachers by Community National Bank.

The new PE teachers are teaching the new state-approved curriculum. They also started a Family Fitness Night once a month. Students bring their families for a night of fitness activities, aerobic homework, and nutrition information. This year, an editor of a women's sports magazine and a former men's Olympic gold medal swimmer spoke as part of the evening program. When asked by one of the new PE teachers to help at the next family night, Stu, who has not participated in the planning or the implementation of the new family fitness program, responded, "This is a waste of the parents' time. Maybe when you invite a real sports person as a speaker, I'll come to hear him. In the meantime, don't look for me to be there."

The Maple View Teachers' Organization elected Stu as their representative for the school district's professional development committee. He was appointed chair of the committee mainly because of his seniority in the district. Stu was reluctant to serve on the committee because he has a history of conflict with Dr. Barbara Campbell. Fred Cooper, the former assistant principal at the high school, is Stu's best friend. Stu feels that his friend Fred got a raw deal when Barbara Campbell came to the district. Like a lot of other teachers, Stu figured Barbara's promotion to assistant principal at the high school was because of the affirmative action program and the new laws about hiring minorities. Now that Barbara is the assistant superintendent for curriculum and staff development and in charge of the staff development budget for the district, Stu knows he will have to work with her. He also resents that the committee meetings are held in the summer, so he and Beverly have to delay their departure for their summer vacation until after the committee meetings are over.

■ Cynthia Hanford Carlson

Ed had added two very active community members to his list. He met Cynthia Hanford Carlson at a community event about a year ago. Cynthia is a long-time resident of Maple View. Her retired father, Robert Hanford, was principal of the old Maple View High School when it had a state football championship three years in a row. She is 42 years old, and with her husband, Don Carlson, has four children attending local schools. Don is the manager of the local Target store.

Cynthia is the newly appointed manager of Human Resources and Customer Service at the Community National Bank (CNB). The bank is located in one of the oldest buildings in the heart of downtown. Three branch offices are located west of the city and one branch is located on the East Side of downtown. Cynthia coordinated CNB's annual "Read for Life" project in conjunction with the public library and the local school district.

Cynthia's current assignment as human resources manager is at the downtown "main office." The training center for the bank's employee development programs is also located in the downtown facility. Cynthia's responsibilities include providing training programs for all new hires, training the on-site trainers, and responding to last-resort customer complaints. Because she knows the community so well, the CEO of the bank felt she would be the best person to resolve customer complaints. In addition to her full-time job, Cynthia volunteers to serve as director of community education for the local Chamber of Commerce. She sees a need for the city to "pull together and pool our resources so that the new residents are better connected to the city's history and that both the old and new can be provided opportunities for growth."

■ Carlos Montanaro

The second community member whom Ed chose to interview was Carlos, a fair-complexioned, 45-year-old Mexican American. Carlos owns and operates the Maple View Rock and Cement Company. His father started the company 25 years ago, and even though Carlos grew up learning the business, his father insisted that Carlos go to college and learn how to make the business even more successful. After Carlos graduated from business school, he became the general manager of the company and took over running it when his father became seriously ill 5 years ago. Under Carlos's leadership, the company has excelled and recently won the Baldridge Business Award, given by a nationally recognized total quality management awards program. Carlos values education and training and wants to be part of the city's leadership training program, Leadership Maple View.

Carlos's wife, Anita, also age 45, is a homemaker and serves as the Pine Hills High School PTA president. Their son, Tony, is in the 11th grade and is the star quarterback for the high school team. Tony wants to attend State University on a full athletic scholarship, but he needs tutoring in math and English. Carlos and Anita do not understand why the teachers and principal at the high school are not doing more to help Tony be successful in the classroom. Despite his 2.0 grade point average, his counselor assures Tony that he will have "no trouble at all" getting into State University with an athletic scholarship.

⟻

Sam and Ed sat at Sam's kitchen table and compared their notes. They were beginning to put the story together, piece by piece, person by person. Ed looked across the table at Sam, "So is it making sense now?"

"Well I'm not sure that I see the whole picture, but I'm beginning to put it together," Sam responded, still reviewing his notes. "I think we have a wonderful opportunity to bring folks together around this issue of the 'East Side secret,' don't you?" Sam asked Ed.

"Yeah, I guess so. But the first thing you have to do is to tell this story to the community. We have to get the facts out there so that as a community we can come together and solve our own problems. We can't afford to keep these secrets any longer. It's the kids who will suffer in the long run," Ed pleaded with Sam.

"You're right, Ed. I think our community leadership project is going to be about learning from and listening to one another. I think we need to ask Dr. Campbell to help us get a better understanding of this cultural proficiency thing. It offers us a different way to approach our concerns around equity and diversity as the city continues to grow. I'll make an appointment with her tomorrow, and we can get started on this project right away." Sam couldn't contain his enthusiasm.

"Thanks for asking me to take this journey with you, Sam. This means a lot to me and my children." Ed reached out to Sam and the intended handshake turned quickly to a bear hug between two new friends.

⟶

Sam Brewer sat at his computer and pounded out the story of the "East Side Secret." The story's setting was familiar to him. Even though names had been changed for the purpose of the article, the characters were real people to Sam. Most important, the issues were real issues facing a community grappling with culture, equity, identity, power, and distribution of resources. For Sam, these were also issues that teachers face daily in their classrooms. Writing Maple View's story gave Sam insights into his own story. He assessed his own culture, examined his own values for diversity, learned to manage the dynamics of difference in his classroom and community, and was learning new ways to adapt to the ever-changing world in which he lives and works. With each day and each new situation, Sam is becoming a culturally proficient instructor.

⟶

The following chapters continue the stories of the teachers and learners of Maple View. We encourage you to go beyond these stories, however, to apply the methods of culturally proficient instruction to your own teaching and learning environment. In these chapters, you'll find numerous opportunities to apply culturally proficient instruction to your own teaching. We encourage you to fully engage yourself with these exercises. Try out the ideas suggested, and give yourself an opportunity to develop your own teaching tools. Once you've tried these ideas for yourself, then evaluate how well they suit your own individual style of teaching. You may readily apply some of them to your current teaching and learning environment. You may need to adapt some others to suit your current situation, and you may find that still others apply less readily to your current situation, but you may be glad to know of them at some future time, when your situation changes.

As with anything in life, you'll find that the more fully you engage yourself with the text and with the suggested activities, the more you'll gain from the experience.

What Is Cultural Proficiency?

*I think the Golden Rule means taking
the time to find out how other people
want to be treated and treating them
that way.*

Getting Centered

Have you ever wondered why a learner comes into your classroom with an attitude? Have you ever wished that you didn't have to deal with the parents of your learners because they are so hard to get along with? Recall and describe one difficult incident that you had recently.

_____

_____

_____

_____

_____

_____

━

Activity

The following list of seven words and descriptions shows how a person may experience a particular social setting. Read each word and its description, then tell about a time when you experienced each particular social phenomenon. You may not have experienced all of them, so you may want to complete this activity in a group. As your colleagues tell their stories, notice the emotions associated with each social phenomenon.

Alienation: Feeling out of place, not fitting in, not belonging to any group.

Example: Being the only single man at a pregnancy support group.

What is a situation in which you or someone you know felt alienated?

_____

_____

_____

_____

_____

What were your feelings (or your colleague's feelings) while in that situation?

_____

_____

_____

_____

_____

_____

Dissonance: Discord, disharmony, feeling out of sync, offbeat, out of tune with your surroundings.

Example: Attending a workshop announced in a professional newsletter, titled "Achieve Your Full Teaching Potential," which turns out to be a meeting to promote a multilevel marketing business that sells educational materials.

What is a situation in which you or someone you know felt dissonance?

_____

_____

_____

_____

_____

_____

What were your feelings (or your colleague's feelings) while in that situation?

_____

_____

_____

_____

_____

_____

_____

Marginality: Identifying with two groups but not fitting in either; being rejected by both groups and relegated to the margins.

Example: Being a biracial person who is rejected by one group because she looks like she belongs to the other group, and by the other group because her values and language are more similar to the first group.

What is a situation in which you or someone you know felt marginalized?

_____

_____

_____

_____

_____

_____

_____

What were your feelings (or your colleague's feelings) while in that situation?

_____

_____

_____

_____

_____

_____

_____

Dualism: Being involved in two cultures and having to hide that fact from one of the cultural groups.

Example: Being a closeted Gay person who works in a straight world.

What is a situation in which you or someone you know experienced dualism?

_____

_____

_____

_____

_____

_____

What were your feelings (or your colleague's feelings) while in that situation?

_____

_____

_____

_____

_____

_____

_____

Negotiation for acceptance: Having to justify being in a particular role or environment, when other people question whether you deserve it.

Example: Being a Latina who is told that the only reason she got a particular position was through affirmative action, then having to prove that she can perform the responsibilities of the job.

What is a situation in which you or someone you know had to negotiate for acceptance?

_____

_____

_____

_____

_____

_____

What were your feelings (or your colleague's feelings) while in that situation?

_____

_____

_____

_____

_____

_____

_____

Bicultural affirmation: Belonging to two cultural groups, with both groups knowing and appreciating your membership in the other group.

Example: *Being a conservative Jew, observant of Jewish law, and keeping kosher while working in an organization dominated by Christians and Christian cultural norms.*

What is a situation in which you or someone you know experienced bicultural affirmation?

_____

_____

_____

_____

_____

_____

_____

What were your feelings (or your colleague's feelings) while in that situation?

_____

_____

_____

_____

_____

_____

_____

Multicultural transformation: Interacting with people from several different cultures over time, with all participants being changed for the better because of the experience.

Example: Attending a Brotherhood-Sisterhood camp for several weeks during the summer; youths meet and develop relationships with other young people of different ethnicities, religions, and nationalities; they learn from one another and are changed dramatically by their experience; they leave camp with a broader understanding and appreciation of people who differ from them.

What is a situation in which you or someone you know experienced multicultural transformation?

_____

_____

_____

_____

_____

_____

What were your feelings (or your colleague's feelings) while in that situation?

_____

_____

_____

_____

_____

_____

_____

⟿

Reflection

Notice how the stories you and your colleagues have been telling stir deeply felt emotions. Think back to the problem situation you described in the "Getting Centered" activity at the beginning of this chapter. Did you notice any similar feelings? Is it possible that the person who was causing the problem for you may have felt alienated, marginalized, or another negative social phenomenon? Did you hear many stories that told of bicultural affirmation or multicultural transformation? Imagine what it would be like if, in your classroom, you and your learners were able to create experiences of multicultural transformation—every time you taught.

_____

_____

_____

_____

_____

_____

_____

Our Vision of Multicultural Transformation

Through this book, we hope to share with you our vision of multicultural transformation. We believe that this transformation can occur if the teacher, professor, or trainer engages in culturally proficient instruction. As we mentioned previously, *cultural proficiency* is the combination of organizational policies and practices or an individual's values and behavior that enables the organization or the person to interact effectively in culturally diverse settings. Culturally proficient instructors—

and organizations—do not necessarily know all there is to know about every cultural group. They do, however, acquire the knowledge, skills, and attitudes that enable them to find out what they need to know, to learn that information, and to use it effectively.

■ What Is Culture?

In describing cultural proficiency, we are defining the term cultural very broadly. For us, *culture* is the set of common beliefs and practices that a person shares with a group. These beliefs and practices identify that person as part of the group, and they help other group members to recognize that person as one of them. Most individuals identify with one or two groups very strongly—this is their dominant culture. They may also identify in a lesser way with other cultural groups. Often, when the word *culture* is used, the listener (or reader) imagines an ethnic culture.

Ethnic cultures are groups of people who are united by ancestry, language, physiology, and history, as well as by their beliefs and practices. In addition to ethnic cultures, there are *corporate cultures*—the culture associated with a particular organization. In a corporate environment, each industry has its own distinctive culture (compare the automotive industry with the film industry), as does each particular company in that industry (compare Saturn with Ford). Within a given company, each of the various departments has its own culture—think about the culture within an accounting department and contrast that with the research-and-development department's culture. Within a school district, the overarching culture of the district distinguishes it from other similar districts. In addition, individual schools have their own distinctive cultures, as do individual classrooms.

Clearly, all these groups and subgroups have much in common, but in many ways, these groups—and their group members—show significant distinctions. Consider the images evoked by these groups: America Online (AOL) versus EarthLink, classified personnel versus certificated teachers, administrators versus faculty, engineers versus human resource personnel, New York City versus Peoria, Illinois. These pairings reflect the cultural differences within a larger cultural group. AOL and EarthLink both provide e-mail services and access to the Internet. Classified and certificated personnel both work in school districts. Administrators and faculty members are both found on a university campus. Engineers and human resource personnel may work for the same company, but their approaches to the people and the work may be as different as New York City is from Peoria, Illinois.

Yet someone who knows the culture of any of these groupings would be able to tell who belonged and who didn't. Culture is about *groupness*. Cultural identity is what enables people to recognize where they belong. Across continents and across time, people have made fundamental distinctions between *us* and *them*. As people in the 21st century, we have retained this human tendency to want to distinguish us from them—our tribe from others—even when doing so hurts both us and them. (Pick your favorite contemporary or ancient archenemies to illustrate this point.) A culturally proficient approach to instruction helps us to overcome this tendency by helping instructors to see and manage the differences in their classrooms.

▪ What Are Some Common Terms Related to Cultural Proficiency?

⟾

Activity

Read the definitions for these commonly used and misused terms. Reflect on each definition, comparing it with what you thought the definition was. Following each one, write about how the definition affirms, helps to clarify, or challenges your thinking.

Culture: Everything you believe and everything you do that identifies you as a member of a group and distinguishes you from members of other groups. You may belong to more than one cultural group. Cultures reflect the belief systems and behaviors informed by ethnicity, as well as by other sociological factors, such as gender, age, sexual orientation, and physical ability. Both individuals and organizations are defined by their cultures.

_____

_____

_____

_____

_____

_____

Affirmative action: A legally mandated approach to increasing the diversity of an organization that focuses on having a proportional representation of all the people in the community within the organization. The intention is to ensure the inclusion of qualified people, but the implementation often results in a focus on counting numbers rather than assessing qualifications.

Multiculturalism: The preservation of different cultures or cultural identities within a society or nation, holding each as equally valuable to and influential on the members of the society. The educational term *multicultural* refers to teaching about different cultures. Multiculturalism differs from cultural proficiency in that it reflects a state of being, whereas cultural proficiency is a process.

Tolerance: Enduring the presence of people who differ from you, or ideas that conflict with yours. Tolerance is the first in a progression of steps that may lead to valuing diversity. Teaching tolerance is a more positive approach to diversity than is genocide or cultural destructiveness, but it is only the beginning of a process that moves toward valuing differences.

_____

_____

_____

_____

_____

_____

_____

Diversity: Diversity is a general term indicating that people who differ from one another are present in an organization or group. It refers to ethnicity, language, gender, age, ability, sexual orientation, and all other aspects of culture.

_____

_____

_____

_____

_____

_____

_____

Politically correct: A term used to describe language or behavior that reflects sensitivity to the diversity of a group. People can *act as if* they are culturally proficient by using politically correct language. A culturally proficient person may be perceived as politically correct, but in reality, that person is *culturally correct*.

_____

_____

_____

_____

_____

_____

_____

Cultural proficiency: The policies and practices of an organization or the values and behaviors of an individual that enable the organization or person to interact effectively in a culturally diverse environment; reflected in the way an organization treats its employees, its clients, and its community; an inside-out approach to issues arising from diversity; a focus on learning about oneself and recognizing how one's culture and one's identity may affect others, not on learning about others.

_____

_____

_____

_____

_____

_____

Culturally proficient instruction: Being a culturally proficient instructor means learning about oneself in a cultural context and creating an environment in which the learners are invited to explore the cultural contexts for who they are and how they respond and relate to one another.

_____

_____

_____

_____

_____

_____

_____

_____

Cultural proficiency is an approach to dealing with the issues arising from diversity. The approach was first described by Terry Cross in his seminal work on cultural competence (see Cross, Bazron, Dennis, & Isaacs, 1993). We are deeply indebted to Dr. Cross for his continuing work in the field of social services and his generosity in endorsing our work as we have applied his concepts to education and industry. Cultural proficiency offers a model—a framework—for developing oneself and one's organization while seeking to address issues of diversity. The cultural-proficiency model is guided by the following principles:

1. **Culture is a predominant force in people's lives.**
2. **People are served in varying degrees by the dominant culture.**
3. **People have personal identities and group identities.**
4. **Diversity within cultures is vast and significant.**
5. **Each group has unique cultural needs.**

The following section introduces you to these principles.

GUIDING PRINCIPLES OF CULTURAL PROFICIENCY

Stuart Montgomery remarked to Charlene Brennaman, "Why do we have to waste time going to this diversity training program? I really don't think it helps the situation when we focus on differences. After all, when you get right down to it, the differences don't really make a difference. We are all people— human beings who get out of bed one leg at a time. If I treat people according to the Golden Rule, I'll be just fine."

Charlene snapped, "That's the problem with you, Stu. You don't understand that the Golden Rule is usually misinterpreted."

"What do you mean?" Stu asked innocently.

"Well, you probably think the Golden Rule means to treat others the way you want to be treated. That interpretation assumes that everyone wants to be treated your way. I think it means taking the time to find out how the other person wants to be treated and treating them that way."

"You aren't making any sense," said Stu.

"Look at you and your wife," Charlene continued. "You want to hear the truth, whether it hurts your feelings or not. You want people to cut through the BS and just give you the bottom line on whatever the topic is. Your wife, on the other hand, is a sensitive person. She doesn't necessarily want you to sugarcoat things, but courtesy and sensitivity to the feelings of others are very important to her. That's why she works in human resources while you are more comfortable with your approach to coaching. You get along much better when you are in control."

"Oh, you're killing me," Stu laughed. "Why don't you just stab me in the heart?"

"Because I am telling you the truth," said Charlene.

"I know that you're right; I just hate to admit it."

"Well finish eating your humble pie," Charlene said, "and get ready to go to our training."

The guiding principles of cultural proficiency are fundamental to the multicultural transformation we defined earlier in this chapter. These guiding principles are attitudinal benchmarks. These foundational values of cultural proficiency are essential for responding to the diversity in your classroom, or in your world, with more than a superficial acknowledgment that differences exist.

Principle 1: Culture Is a Predominant Force

You cannot *not* have a culture. Therefore, as an instructor, it is important to acknowledge culture as a predominant force in shaping behaviors, values, and institutions. Culture determines how you interact with your learners and react to things that happen in the classroom. Cultural biases invite you to judge behavior that differs from yours. Cultural differences are sometimes the cause of behaviors in others that you might find offensive. The organizational norms, the school climate, and the unwritten rules of your organization are all a reflection of its culture. Remember that culture is about groupness, not just ethnicity. Culture is the set of beliefs and behaviors of any group that distinguishes the group.

Reflection

List aspects of culture—yours and your learners'—that affect how your lessons are received.

_____

_____

_____

_____

_____

_____

_____

_____

While reflecting on organizations in which you have worked, describe an organizational policy or practice that affirms this guiding principle.

_____

_____

_____

_____

_____

_____

Describe an instructional behavior of yours or of someone you know that illustrates this principle.

_____

_____

_____

_____

_____

_____

_____

_____

■ Principle 2: People Are Served in Varying Degrees by the Dominant Culture

If you are a member of the dominant culture, you may not even notice the many ways that the culture of your organization or group affects those who do not know the cultural norms or rules. What works for you in your classroom, your organization, and your community may work against members of other cultural groups. Often, when members of dominant cultures recognize that there are cultural differences, they suggest that the persons in nondominant cultures simply change and learn the new rules. This approach puts the burden for change on just the nondominant groups. A commitment to cultural proficiency is a commit- ment to a dynamic relationship in which all parties learn from one another and adapt as they adjust to their differences.

Reflection

What works for the dominant culture of your organization or school that may not work for all its employees or students?

_____

_____

_____

_____

_____

_____

_____

_____

_____

_____

While reflecting on organizations in which you have worked, describe an organizational policy or practice that affirms this guiding principle.

_____

_____

_____

_____

_____

_____

Describe an instructional behavior of yours or of someone you know that illustrates this principle.

_____

_____

_____

_____

_____

_____

_____

_____

Principle 3: People Have Personal Identities and Group Identities

Although it is important to treat all people as individuals, it is also important to acknowledge the group identity of individuals. You cannot guarantee the dignity of a person unless you also preserve the dignity of his or her people. Making negative comments or reinforcing a negative stereotype about the group is insulting to its members. Moreover, attempting to separate the person from her or his group by telling the person, "You're different; you're not like those other XXXs," is offensive and denies that the person may identify strongly with other XXXs.

Reflection

List some words and phrases that might insult or discount members of cultural groups in your organization.

_____

_____

_____

_____

_____

_____

_____

_____

_____

_____

_____

While reflecting on organizations in which you have worked, describe an organizational policy or practice that affirms this guiding principle.

_____

_____

_____

_____

_____

_____

_____

Describe an instructional behavior of yours or of someone you know that illustrates this principle.

_____

_____

_____

_____

_____

_____

_____

⟿

▪ Principle 4: Diversity Within Cultures Is Vast and Significant

Because diversity within cultures is as important as diversity among cultures, it is important to learn about cultural groups, not as monoliths—such as women, Asians, and Gay men—but as the complex and diverse groups of individuals that they are. In the United States, each of the major ethnic and cultural groups is also divided along class lines. There are poor, working-class, middle-class, and upper-class people among all the groups. Stereotypes about particular groups give the impression that all members of a group share the socioeconomic status of some—or even most—members of the group. For example, some people believe that all African Americans are poor and undereducated. Sociological literature (Gordon, 1978; Myrdal, 1944) informs us that when examining lifestyle and values, upper-class African Americans share more in common with upper-class European Americans than they do with poor African Americans. These class similarities can be found across cultural lines among most groups in the United States. Consequently, Principle 4 reminds us of the diversity within groups, as well as between them.

⟞

Reflection

What are some of the subgroups of the major cultures represented in your organization? How might the differences within groups affect the nature of the conflict you may experience or the way you deliver your instruction or other services?

_____

_____

_____

_____

_____

_____

While reflecting on organizations in which you have worked, describe an organizational policy or practice that affirms this guiding principle.

_____

_____

_____

_____

_____

_____

_____

_____

Describe an instructional behavior of yours or of someone you know that illustrates this principle.

_____

_____

_____

_____

_____

_____

_____

_____

⟿

■ Principle 5: Each Group Has Unique Cultural Needs

Each cultural group has unique needs that cannot be met within the boundaries of the dominant culture. When others express their own group's cultural identity, they do not imply a disrespect for yours. Make room in your organization for several paths leading to the same goal. Within your classroom, you probably plan for a variety of learning styles. When you develop a lesson, you consider that some learners need concrete examples; others are more comfortable with abstract ideas. Some learners respond to visual cues, whereas others must be physically engaged before they grasp a concept. People who teach, even if their teaching style favors one mode of learning over another, usually respect differences in how people learn new ideas. Differences in cultural needs also invite acknowledgment and respect from instructors. For example, attitudes toward authority, and deference to seniority in age or tenure, greatly affect the learning climate.

Reflection

What are some of the unique cultural needs you have observed in the learners in your classroom and in your colleagues?

_____

_____

_____

_____

_____

_____

_____

_____

_____

While reflecting on organizations in which you have worked, describe an organizational policy or practice that affirms this guiding principle.

_____

_____

_____

_____

_____

_____

_____

Describe an instructional behavior of yours or of someone you know that illustrates this principle.

_____

_____

_____

_____

_____

_____

_____

⟿

Going Deeper

For the next several days, take note of how people in your professional setting address issues of culture. Note their levels of comfort with conversation about culture and diversity. Pay attention to how people describe colleagues and learners who differ from them. Pay attention to how you describe those who differ from you. The words that you and your colleagues use will give you insight into your values in this area. After a few days, ask yourself, What am I learning about my colleagues, this organization, and myself?

⟿

Essential Elements of Cultural Proficiency

The guiding principles of cultural proficiency are the values that inform the essential elements of cultural proficiency. These elements reflect the specific behaviors fundamental to culturally proficient instruction:

- Assessing culture
- Valuing diversity
- Managing the dynamics of difference
- Adapting to diversity
- Institutionalizing cultural knowledge

These elements are briefly described in this chapter and elaborated in Chapters 6 through 10.

⟿

Reflection

Look over the essential elements of culturally proficient instruction that follow. Which ones will be easy for you to implement? Which ones will be more difficult? What can you do and what resources can you seek to make it easier for you to become a culturally proficient instructor?

Table 3.1 Essential Elements of Cultural Proficiency

■ Assessing Culture

Naming the Differences
- Describing your own culture and the cultural norms of your organization
- Recognizing how your culture affects others
- Understanding how the culture of your organization impacts those whose culture is different

■ Valuing Diversity

Claiming the Differences
- Recognizing difference as diversity, rather than as inappropriate responses to the environment
- Accepting that each culture considers some values and behaviors more important than others
- Seeking opportunities to work with and learn from people who differ from you

■ Managing the Dynamics of Difference

Reframing the Differences
- Understanding the effect of historic distrust on present-day interactions
- Realizing that you may misjudge another's actions based on your own learned expectations
- Learning effective ways to resolve conflicts among people whose culture and values may differ from yours

■ Adapting to Diversity

Training About Differences
- Changing the way you have done things to acknowledge the differences present among staff members, clients, and community members
- Aligning programs and practices with the guiding principles of cultural proficiency
- Institutionalizing appropriate interventions for conflicts and confusion caused by the dynamics of difference

■ Institutionalizing Cultural Knowledge

Changing for Differences
- Incorporating Cultural Knowledge into the mainstream of the organization
- Developing skills for cross-cultural communication
- Integrating into the organization's systems information and skills that enable you to interact effectively in a variety of cultural situations

NOTES

Barriers to Cultural Proficiency

Change will not be effective if you don't clearly know what you are changing from. I can't give you directions until you tell me where you are.

Getting Centered

Think about the last time you were frustrated in your classroom. What was keeping you from doing your best work? What barriers may have kept the learners from doing their best work?

_____

_____

_____

_____

_____

_____

_____

A Sense of Entitlement and Unawareness of the Need to Adapt

In a culturally proficient organization, effective instructors have a profound knowledge about the subject matter, as well as the ability to teach it. At a minimum, they have a well-developed philosophy of teaching and can readily use a wide variety of instructional strategies to convey what they know of the content. Perhaps more important, they effectively interact with learners. From a culturally proficient perspective, however, effective instructors must also have reflected on the barriers to cultural proficiency.

The chief barriers to cultural proficiency are a lack of awareness of the need to adapt and a sense of entitlement. *Being unaware of the need to adapt* means not recognizing the need to make personal and organizational changes in response to the diversity of the people within the learning environment. A person facing such a barrier believes that the only ones who need to change and adapt are the "others"—the ones who are "not like us." A person who has a *sense of entitlement* believes that all the personal achievements and societal benefits that she or he enjoys were accrued solely on her or his individual merit and quality of character.

These barriers emanate from the assumption that the successes a person has enjoyed as an instructor or learner are available to everyone else in the same way they were available to that person. The barriers are built on at least five assumptions: (1) All people have access to knowledge, skills, and attitudes in the same manner and quality; (2) all people in the classroom or training room relate to everyone else the way they related to the instructor when he or she was a learner; (3) it doesn't matter whether the students are members of a historically entitled population (e.g., propertied white men) or of a historically oppressed group; (4) it doesn't matter whether the students are successful in this society (e.g., Latina professional) or are less so (e.g., poor white male high school dropout); and (5) the instructor has tremendous power and equal potential for influence over all the learners in the environment, regardless of the students' background or experiences or current situation.

Most of us have never taken the time to thoroughly examine the basis for our assumptions, values, and beliefs. However, we do recognize when we feel under attack. Our initial response usually is to blindly defend what has always been there. In this society, that is often the case with attitudes toward people who differ from us.

L uAnn Steiner is chairing the first meeting of the Committee for Culturally Proficient Instruction. Several committee members arrived early and are conversing over coffee and cookies while LuAnn and the staff complete the setup for the meeting.

Stu Montgomery, the district representative from the professional development committee, joins the group and observes several posters and quotations placed in the room as part of the environment for the committee meeting: "Look at this room. I guess we're going to hear the 'I Have a Dream' speech again today. I get tired of hearing how bad things are for some groups. It's not my fault that some white families held slaves before the Civil War."

"Nobody said it was your fault, Stu. No need to feel guilty about something we had no control over," Andy replied.

Arlene couldn't let this moment pass. "Well, you two are always defending yourselves. Our black kids need to learn what the real history is so they can make up their own minds about the world, not just learn the one way that you want them to see it."

LuAnn decided that this was a good place to start. "Well, it sounds like we have a lot to talk about today. Cultural proficiency will help us frame our conversations to move beyond the anger and guilt that we feel. Let's get started. While anger or guilt may be normal, if one chooses to stay at that level, it rarely results in deeper learning. However, if it is viewed as an indicator that you are on the verge of deeper learning, it will lead toward cultural proficiency."

Reflection

Take this opportunity to identify some of your own blind spots. Identify a group with which you are not as effective as you would like to be. Perhaps you believe you are not maximally effective with African American women, Latino men, Lesbians, European American men, people with AIDS, or lawyers. Write a brief description of this group. Remember that almost everyone holds stereotypical views of members of other groups.

Now write two or three assumptions or beliefs that you hold about members of that group. For instance, if you select African Americans, you may write that you have doubts about their academic abilities. If you select Gay men and Lesbians, you may write about your perception that they have promiscuous lifestyles. If you select lawyers, you may describe them as money grubbers. Take a few minutes, and write your assumptions and beliefs and what you know to be your biases.

_____

_____

_____

_____

_____

_____

Remember that your assumptions and beliefs serve as filters when working with groups that differ culturally from your own group. Knowing and acknowledging such assumptions and beliefs is an important initial step in the journey toward becoming culturally proficient. Look at your list again, adding to it as more thoughts come to you. Write first, then talk with a trusted colleague. How do you think your beliefs, assumptions, and biases influence the way you teach and the environment you create in your classroom?

_____

_____

_____

_____

_____

_____

⌐⌐

A Short Sociology Lesson

Many people describe U.S. society as a dominant group of "plain Americans" and a diverse group of "minorities." *Minorities* are generally those ethnic and social groups that have a history of oppression in the United States. At the same time, it is important to differentiate two kinds of minorities: *castelike groups*, those whose social status rarely changes (e.g., African Americans and Native Americans), and *oppressed immigrant groups* (e.g., Irish and Italian laborers), who assimilated into dominant society after two or three generations (Ogbu, 1978).

Castelike minorities were brought to the United States against their will or were subjugated during the European migration to North America. As such, these groups endured centuries of legalized racism—slavery, Jim Crow laws, confinement to reservations, and internment camps. Although many people from these groups have been successful in our society, as a group they are overrepresented in the lowest socioeconomic classes, and they are the targets of race-based hatred and discrimination. Oppressed immigrant groups were confined to menial, hard-labor tasks during the 19th and 20th centuries, and like the castelike minorities, they had to resort to legal means to ensure their basic rights. In contrast to the castelike minorities, however, their second and third generations have begun to experience greater success in this country's economic and political arenas.

European immigrant groups also experienced discrimination and deprivation during their first years in the United States. However, European immigrant groups found that as they entered into their second and third generations, they became "white" or "American." These were the Americans who were embraced by the great American melting pot. Although members of castelike groups and oppressed immigrant groups can rightfully point to the hard work their ancestors performed to succeed in the United States (often referred to as "pulling oneself up by one's bootstraps"), European Americans represent the largest proportion of successes—those who moved into the middle and upper social classes in U.S. society. This is the result of hard work, good fortune in some cases, and sometimes the systematic oppression visited on castelike and immigrant groups. Edward Ball (1998) described this process well:

> No one among the Balls talked about how slavery helped us, but whether we acknowledged it or not, the powers of our ancestors were still in hand. Although our social franchise had shrunk, it had nevertheless survived. If we did not inherit money, or land, we received a great fund of cultural capital, including prestige, a

chance at education, self-esteem, a sense of place, mobility, even (in some cases) a flair for giving orders. And it was not only "us," the families of former slave owners, who carried the baggage of the plantations. By skewing things so violently in the past, we had made sure that our cultural riches would benefit all white Americans.

. . . At the same time, the slave business was a crime that had not fully been acknowledged. It would be a mistake to say that I felt guilt for the past. A person cannot be culpable for the acts of others, long dead, that he or she could not have influenced. Rather than responsible, I felt accountable for what had happened, called on to try to explain it. I also felt shame about the broken society that had washed up when the tide of slavery receded. (pp. 13-14)

Ball raises several important concepts. First, he and members of his family benefited from a system that preceded them by generations. It just makes sense that when benefits are denied to one group of people, they accrue to others. Think about it. Those benefits that are denied to one group do not disappear. If one group is systematically denied access to education while other groups have access to education, the latter groups are much more likely to be able to succeed socially and economically.

Second, Ball introduces the concept of guilt. In our workshops, we often observe that when confronted with these ideas for the first time, many people experience guilt or anger. If you are feeling resentful or defensive now, you may be realizing that some of your education has been incomplete. Resentfulness expressed as anger and defensiveness resulting from guilt is a legitimate feeling. Anger and guilt can immobilize you as an instructor and can impede you from seeing your entitlement. Instead, as LuAnn Steiner expressed in the previous vignette, experiencing these very human feelings can indicate you are on the verge of deeper learning. The unrest or discomfort you may feel are signals that you are shifting away from seeking external, stereotypic reasons for why learners are not successful to pursuing an internal focus on what you need to learn to do differently as an instructor.

Now that you have this information, what can you do with it? We do not wish to fan the flames of anger or guilt, but we do want you to consider how this realization informs and forms your practice as an instructor.

Now, we add one final piece to the puzzle. One of the risks in talking about castelike and immigrant minorities is to overlook the fact that large numbers of people from these groups historically have been and currently are very successful. They are well educated, have socially prominent positions, possess modest to great wealth, and have significant political influence in regions of the country. Sadly, when successful members of minority groups are in control of organizations, it is not unusual for these organizations to discriminate actively against members of other minority groups.

The focus of this book is on you, the instructor. Whether you are a member of the dominant group or you are from a minority group, you possess great power as an instructor. As such, you participate in the dominant group and need to be aware of how you potentially hinder or facilitate the learning of others. This ability emanates from your power as an instructor. Whether you are a member of an entitled or a historically oppressed group, you have the capacity and the responsibility to reach out to all learners.

S usie Cheng, a newly appointed human relations specialist, is conducting a workshop on conflict resolution for department heads at Tri Cities Community College. She asks the group, "What is your role in resolving conflicts that originate from cultural misunderstandings in the workplace?"

Alan, a science instructor, says "I never really see any conflicts like that among my students. They just come to class to learn."

Carter, an English instructor says, "Sometimes my students write about how they don't like other students because of their lifestyles or values. I just don't make it a topic of discussion during class."

Olivia, who teaches history, adds "Suzie, by asking the question the way that you did, you must have some insight into the role that we as faculty have in resolving conflict. Do you really think we can make much difference with students when they don't get along with students or groups who are different?"

Suzie is glad for the chance to explain: "The principle of unintended consequences is at play here. Even though one does not intend to harm another, or to benefit from the harm done to another, when viewed from a systemic process, most of us benefit from the discrimination visited on others in unintentional and unacknowledged ways. The object lesson here is to see, to know, and to experience how one benefits. At the same time, it is important to realize that these benefits accrue in the complete absence of intention and are, usually, so much a part of our life that we are not aware of it."

⟼

Reflection

What are you thinking and feeling now?

_____

_____

_____

_____

_____

_____

_____

⟼

Language of Entitlement as a Barrier For Instructors

Stereotypes about castelike and immigrant groups abound in classrooms and training rooms. Our language is a key to understanding how we have been shaped to have certain views. The training room and the school classroom exist in an institutional framework that has not served all students well. Those of us who live and work in these settings have been influenced by societally held assumptions, values, and beliefs about other cultural groups. To fully understand how entitlement creates barriers for some and opportunities for others, you need to see how your language objectifies and dehumanizes people. Language reflects the power relationships in our society. Historically, our society has used language to explain the disparities between oppressed and entitled groups (Lindsey, Nuri Robins, & Terrell, 1999). Chart 4.1 presents some common terms reflecting these disparities.

Each of the terms in the first column describes groups that occupy the oppressed end of the entitlement continuum. These terms are used to explain why students from these groups fail to perform at specified levels. Using these terms gives instructors permission to view a learner, and

CHART 4.1 *Words Used to Describe Oppressed and Entitled Groups*

Oppressed	Entitled
Disadvantaged	Advantaged
Culturally disadvantaged	Culturally advantaged
Educationally disadvantaged	Educationally advantaged
Different	Alike
Deficient	Superior
Culturally deprived	Culturally superior
Third World	First World
Minority	Majority
Underclass	Upper class
Diverse	Uniform
Poor	Middle class
Laborers	Leaders

that person's group, as not being able to achieve. Similarly, these terms free the instructor from considering the institutionalized oppression to which these learners are subjected. It makes it so simple. *They* (whoever *they* are) are not learning because they are incapable of doing so. The unquestioned use of these terms suggests that people of color, who are disproportionately represented on the oppressed end of the continuum, suffer from pathological conditions. Unfortunately, this polarity of language and perceptions emanates daily from schools and training rooms.

The effect of using terms of oppression is that the focus is on what is wrong with *them*, implying that these "others" must be studied and then fixed. The terms in the second column, when applied in classrooms and training rooms, describe learners who are part of the dominant culture of our country. The instructor who aspires to be culturally proficient looks at the words in the second column and examines the implications of those terms being used or inferred when interacting with learners who represent the dominant group in our society. That these words are rarely spoken underscores the fact that entitled people do not objectify or name themselves. They only name *others*, people they perceive to differ from themselves.

The use of the terms *disadvantaged* and *deprived,* in their many permutations, implies that there is a norm to which people are compared (Lindsey et al., 1999). There are at least two considerations here. One is that norms are fixed and immutable and that any person or group that fails to measure up to that norm must be deficient in some way. The other is the belief on the part of middle-class America that all groups want to be like them, when many may not. Many groups don't want to do what they perceive as "acting white" (Singham, 1998). The limitation in each of these explanations is that the focus of change is on the learner and not on the instructor. When the focus is on instruction rather than on the perceived, stereotypic capabilities of the learner, achievement results (Haycock, 1998; Noguera, 1999; Singham, 1998).

Once instructors take the responsibility to examine their own behaviors, as Suzie Cheng invites us to do in the previous vignette, then significant progress can be made in identifying institutional barriers and making instructional decisions to benefit learners.

Institutional Barriers to Cultural Proficiency

Culturally proficient instructors have good command of their subject matter and use a variety of teaching techniques. They see each learner as an individual and express to the learner, in myriad ways, their interest in the learner's success and ability to learn. Instructors know the learner's learning style and teach to that style. They also work with the learner to experiment with, and to become comfortable with, alternative learning styles. In doing so, they recognize that the learner needs to know the information and, by facilitating the learner in alternative learning styles, are preparing the learner to succeed in a variety of settings. Culturally proficient corporate trainers or university professors may not have this intimate knowledge of each learner. Nonetheless, they recognize that learning styles differ, and they prepare materials and activities that acknowledge the diverse needs and learning styles of adult learners.

Sam Brewer recognizes that the way life works for him may not be the way it works for others. He recognizes that on his way to the classroom this morning, when he stopped at the local coffee bar for his customary scone and double latte, not everyone was welcomed in the same manner. He knows that as a student, he was above average. His teachers expected him to succeed, and if he had not, they would have contacted his parents. He knows that he had one teacher who saw that he had potential and that this teacher's encouragement contributed mightily to his success. He wants to influence the learners in his classroom in the same way.

⟵

Helen Williams acknowledges that what used to work in classrooms and training rooms may not work in today's diverse settings. She recognizes that, as an African American, she related well to the African American students when they used to live in this community. Now, she recognizes that the demographic shift has presented her with students whose first language is other than English. Though she and her students are both members of "minority" groups, she has lots to learn to be an effective instructor for these new students.

⟵

Suzie Cheng sees that, as a trainer, the lecture presentation style is not as effective with new employees as are more collaborative-cooperative instructional strategies. She has learned that she must adapt to their learning needs. She is engaged in her own continuing learning.

The culturally proficient instructor believes that when new learners experience difficulties, it is not the learners' cultural behaviors and patterns that are suspect, but rather, it is the instructor's behavior that must change and adapt to meet their needs for learning.

⟵

Alicia Alvarez, the director of Training and Staff Development at University Medical Center in Maple View, meets with her supervisor, Alan Roderick, to discuss an upcoming training session. In the past, Alan has given Alicia the topics for the training. This time, he plans to do so again: "Alicia, I think the next training session should be our module, 'Communication Skills for Managers,' like we did last year."

This year, however, Alicia wants to offer a different approach. She says, "I've been thinking about that topic also, Alan. I looked at the feedback forms from the last session that I did, and the participants asked whether we could do something about the topics of conflict resolution and problem solving in their areas of service. I think this is important to consider. As effective instructors, we become students ourselves and, as such, seek new and different ways to meet the needs of the learners with whom we are working."

Alan was thoughtful. "But they each have different areas of service and different kinds of problems. The module is already written and it would be too hard to change it."

Alicia replied, "I've been gathering a variety of materials in each of the service areas. I found a great video that we could use, and we could ask them to create several scenarios about their real problem areas; then we could design activities around those scenarios. I could put a new module together by early next week for you to look at."

"OK, Alicia, I think you are onto something here. Try it."

Instructors must commit ourselves to ensuring constructive outcomes for all learners. Culturally proficient instructors must be able to see the process of teaching and learning from the social context of the learners. An important component of this teaching-learning dynamic is to see the barriers that exist for some, but not all, learners. When instructors acknowledge and consider these barriers in preparing instructional materials, they provide for more equitable learning opportunities.

Six institutional processes can pose barriers to learning unless a culturally proficient instructor, and organization, overcomes these barriers:

1. **Content:** A curriculum that projects only one cultural experience
2. **Delivery:** Instruction that emphasizes lower-order thinking skills (memorization, learning by rote, recitation of the one right answer)
3. **Expectations:** Preconceptions based on stereotypical views of the learners
4. **Assessment:** Evaluation of progress or achievement that is compliance oriented
5. **Resources:** Culturally inadequate resources that continue and maintain inappropriate policies and practices
6. **Outside involvement:** Biased parent and community involvement that caters to the most influential parents and community members; management not included in the design, delivery, or reinforcement of training programs

Activity

As you and your colleagues reflect on your places of instruction, ask yourselves, Who benefits most from these six institutional processes that are barriers to culturally proficient instruction? What have you observed or heard that supports your answers?

_____

_____

_____

_____

_____

_____

_____

Now, think about yourself as a learner. How does a learning environment that has the barriers described suit you as a learner? How does it pose difficulties for you as a learner?

_____

_____

_____

_____

_____

_____

_____

People who have benefited from such systems are often confused by—or openly hostile to—the notion that the system can't necessarily work for anyone who is willing to try harder. They correctly point out that they worked hard for what they have achieved. Because that was their experience, they assume that others must have had the same or similar experiences. That assumption is dangerous and myopic and poses a barrier to culturally proficiency. It reflects a lack of awareness of the need to adapt. In contrast, the culturally proficient instructor feels committed to learning what is necessary to teach others. This instructor is able to take those six institutional practices and modify them in ways that make them work for others, not against them.

🖛

Activity

Review the following six institutional practices. Study the examples, and in the spaces provided, write examples of barriers in your instructional environment for those who differ from the dominant group.

Knowing the barriers to effective instruction greatly empowers you as an instructor. These barriers are grounded in historical events and perpetuated in current institutional policies and practices. Nonetheless, as a culturally proficient instructor, it is your responsibility to make the changes in the domain over which you have the most control and influence: your classroom. When you collaborate with others in how you approach your classrooms, you begin the process of shaping the policies and practices of your organizations.

■ Institutional Practices as Barriers to Instruction

Content Barriers

- Single-perspective curriculum, often represented by a single-text approach
- Curricular program that segregates diversity as a separate course
- Tracking of students into segregated classrooms, where they are given content designed in accord with stereotypes about them
- Use of commercial training materials that aren't customized for a particular classroom and group of students

_____

_____

_____

_____

_____

Delivery Barriers

- Emphasis on basic skills only
- Passive, teacher-directed learning (i.e., lectures)
- Failure to learn students' names
- Failure to learn how to pronounce students' names

_____

_____

_____

_____

Expectation Barriers

- Use of models emphasizing innate ability (e.g., bell curve and norm fallacies) instead of efficacy
- Different instruction based on ability grouping
- Expecting training programs to fix whatever problems the managers have identified
- Using training to punish employees for inappropriate behavior
- Using training as an alternative to adequate supervision and coaching on the job

_____

_____

_____

_____

Assessment Barriers
- Reliance on text and basic-skills approach
- Little feedback to learners during the course
- Data used for compliance purposes, not to inform practice
- Failures reported to the managers, not to the learners
- Assumptions about "appropriate" learner responses

Resource Barriers

- Controlled access to gifted and talented education (GATE) and to advanced placement (AP) instruction
- In colleges and universities, majors associated with a particular culture or gender
- Limited access to extracurricular activities
- Use of paper-and-pen materials rather than the wider range of materials that speaks to diverse learning styles
- Training budgets so small that training departments exist in name only
- Constraints on workers, either failing to release them for training or making training an onerous addition to their workload because no one else can do their jobs

---

Barriers to Organizational or Community Involvement

- Belief that parents who don't come to school must not care
- Activist parents being considered antischool or even anti-education
- Lack of services from or involvement with the local community
- Supervisors who send workers to training to "fix" them
- Executive management totally unaware of the training programs being offered

_____

_____

_____

_____

_____

_____

_____

Going Deeper

Over the next few weeks, observe the institutional barriers in the organizations you encounter (e.g., a store, hospital, bank, school, university, etc.) that may impede the involvement of all interested parties. Note the examples you find.

_____

_____

_____

_____

_____

NOTES

5

The Cultural Proficiency Continuum

For change to be effective, you must begin where you and your organization are, not where you want yourself or your organization to be.

The cultural proficiency continuum provides a context, or frame of reference, by which you can examine organizations and individuals. You can use the cultural proficiency continuum as a tool for analyzing your organizational culture as well as your personal approach to issues of diversity. In an organizational context, you can use the continuum to examine and understand how your organization implements and enforces existing policies and practices. On a personal level, you can use it to describe specific events as expressions of your instructional values and behaviors.

The continuum may help you to delve more deeply into your organization's prevailing policies and practices, as well as their rationale, to reveal more about your organization's culture. For instance, in a given school or classroom, responses to the following questions, based on the continuum, would yield rich information about its prevailing culture:

- When achievement is examined by subgroup (e.g., gender, race, or ethnicity), are learners succeeding similarly across groups?
- Does the examination of instructor-learner response patterns across subgroups reveal differences in frequency of, duration of, or prompts for higher-level thinking?
- Will all learners find themselves represented in the curriculum?

Good

Responses to questions such as these allow us to better understand the learning environment that students experience. The resulting responses provide rich information about the organization or classroom culture. Similarly, continuing self-examination will provide you with the opportunity to examine your own policies, de facto practice, and behaviors that include some learners and exclude others. In this way, you may assess how you act out your own inherited and acquired values and behaviors.

We urge you to carefully review this continuum before proceeding to the chapters on the essential elements of cultural proficiency. We have found in our work with people who are learning to use the cultural-proficiency model that they are better able to effectively apply the essential elements of cultural proficiency to their own classrooms and organizations *after* they have had an opportunity to understand the cultural-proficiency continuum. By understanding and internalizing the continuum in its deepest implications, you will be better able to appreciate and understand this important dynamic of organizational change. For change to be effective, you must begin where you and your organization are, not where you want yourself or your organization to be.

In applying the continuum to your own instruction or organization, we urge you not to use it to label yourself or your organization at fixed points; human and organizational cultures are too complex to be relegated to fixed points. Each organization and instructor can usually be represented at a range of points on the continuum—points that vary with the situations in which they find themselves. While avoiding overall labels, use the continuum to study singular events in your classroom or in your organization, to examine specific policies or particular behaviors, or to analyze your organizational culture or your personal development. In doing so, use the range of points as starting places and benchmarks by which to assess progress and direction. Bear in mind, however, that your movement along the continuum will not be a fluid progression continually gliding along in the right direction. As with all other aspects of learning, you'll experience fits and starts, great leaps forward, occasional slides backward, and jerky half-hearted movements ahead again.

Six Phases of the Cultural Proficiency Continuum

The continuum comprises six phases of organizational life or personal development. The continuum begins with its most negative phase, cultural destructiveness, then proceeds to the less violent phases of cultural incapacity and cultural blindness, and then moves to the more positive

and constructive phases of cultural precompetence, cultural competence, and cultural proficiency (see Figure 5.1). In this chapter, we use
vignettes to illustrate the major concepts at each of the six points along
the continuum.

■ Cultural Destructiveness

Cultural destructiveness is any policy, practice, or behavior that effectively eliminates all vestiges of other people's cultures; it may be mani-
fested through an organization's policies and practices or through an
individual's values and behaviors. Sometimes, these destructive actions
occur intentionally, but more often, they are unwittingly carried out as
part of prevailing practice. Systems of legalized oppression are clear
examples. Legalized oppression includes the system of slavery that
accompanied the African diaspora, Jim Crow laws of segregation, the
reservation system established and maintained for Native American
Indians, the boarding school system that forced Native American children to be separated from their families, the internment of Japanese
American citizens during World War II, and the many means by which
people have been denied the use of their native languages.

In addition to these egregious examples are less obvious, but no less
pernicious, instances of cultural destructiveness. For instance, history
textbooks used in some of the most prominent school districts do little to
explain the origins of modern racism. Thankfully, they do a better job
than the textbooks of the 1950s and 1960s in revealing the historical
racism underlying the enslavement of Africans and African Americans
and the subjugation of Native Americans. Nonetheless, current textbooks still do little to link historical racism to its modern counterpart.
The effects of modern racism on people of color is generally well
described, but most textbooks do little to link modern racism to historical white complicity in the perpetuation of racism. According to a
respected analyst of history textbooks, James Loewen (1995), the expla-
nation of this link from history to today would give students a perspective on "what caused racism in the past, what perpetuates it today, and
how it might be reduced in the future" (p. 138).

In these cases of more subtle forms of cultural destructiveness, textbook authors and other educators fail to show the numerous benefits
that members of the dominant society have derived from the subjugation
of other people. As a result, members of the dominant group do not
know the link between history and modern events, so they readily avoid
becoming involved in eliminating contemporary systems of oppression.
Thus, cultural destructiveness not only perpetuates the negative effects

Figure 5.1. *The Cultural Proficiency Continuum*

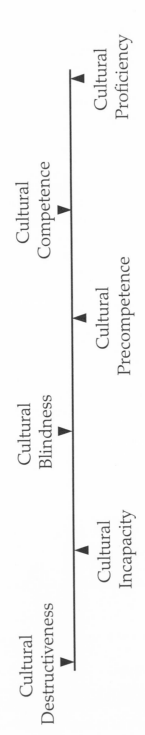

of oppression on nondominant groups but also seems to justify a distorted view of reality on the part of groups that benefit from these same systems of oppression.

Another aspect of cultural destructiveness is the absence of many ✓ people and events in most school curricula, which leads to the question, "What happened to our history and literature books?" Whether intentional or unintentional, when textbook authors and curriculum developers omit entirely or neglect or distort the contributions of entire cultural groups, they are engaging in cultural destructiveness.

Some people worry that to raise these issues, is to engage in divisiveness and negativity. That reaction only perpetuates cultural destructiveness. Just as we don't help alcoholics by denying their alcohol-related problems and behavior, it doesn't help our nation to heal its divisions by ignoring entire cultures or cultural groups. Though one may try to ignore these problems, they continue to pose a source of concern and embarrassment.

The oppression of people of color and other nondominant groups in the United States damages society. At present, the dominant society often appears to be unaware of the need to adapt and respond to the many incidents of oppression that exist. This denial tears at the moral fiber of U.S. society.

To deny the experiences of all members of society is to deny the barriers to cultural proficiency discussed in the previous chapter. Acknowledging these barriers is not to deny or excuse current efforts at accomplishment. Rather, to recognize barriers creates opportunities to learn for members of both the dominant group and the nondominant or "minority" groups. In doing so, members of the dominant group become aware of the unacknowledged benefits they derive from systems of oppression and then choose to accept their personal responsibility for perpetuating those systems as a way of life. Members of "minority" groups become fully aware of these systems and choose not to be perpetual victims; they fully understand the oppression that arises from being viewed, by themselves and by others, as victims, and instead, they choose self-determination as a way of life.

Research

For more examples of cultural destructiveness, please read the following books: Andrews and Gates (1999), Carmichael and Hamilton (1967), Franklin and Moss (1988), Lindsey (1999), Loewen (1995), Ogbu (1978), Takaki (1993), and Vigil (1980). (The full references for each are given at the end of this book.) Each of these works may extend your understanding of the historical dynamics that have led to the many current, unresolved issues related to diversity. These unresolved issues beg to be addressed by those who aspire to cultural proficiency.

⟜

Reflection

Write your reaction to what you have just read. List additional examples of cultural destructiveness.

_____

_____

_____

_____

_____

_____

_____

⟜

In an 11th-grade course in the humanities, combining U.S. history and literature, the teacher, Ms. Linda Catelli, has had the
students read _Voyage of the Damned_ and _Judgment at Nuremberg_.
Her goal is to have the students develop an understanding of the
horrors of war. She plans, next week, to use the video _Saving Private Ryan_.

"Well, in these last two weeks we have covered a lot of information! Some of it, I am sure, you found troubling," said Ms.
Catelli.

"You know, Ms. Catelli," said Tom, "I think you believe all
this BS, but I am here to tell you that either the holocaust did not
happen or if it did, the international Jewish conspiracy has blown
it way out of proportion!"

"What the hell is the international Jewish conspiracy?"
Adrian squealed. "You sound like some kind of nut!"

"Hey, who are you calling a nut?" Tom retorted. "Haven't
you heard of the New World Order?"

"Tom! Adrian! Knock it off, you two," pleaded Ms. Catelli, trying to regain order. "I am tired of you two arguing during every single class. Tom, where did you ever get such outrageous ideas?"

"On the Internet!" Tom raged. "I am tired of the biased information that we get in this school. It is always about how so-called minorities have been exploited. I have a couple of Web sites that tell the real history. Did you know that Hitler was only trying to preserve a way of life, and communists and Jews were undermining that way of life? Did you know that Martin Luther King was a communist dedicated to the overthrow of our country? Did you know that the welfare system is the way that minorities are undermining the economy of this country? Did you know that I can study hard and graduate from this damned school, but I won't be able to get a job because I am the wrong color, sex, and religion?"

⟶

Activity

What are the issues of cultural destructiveness in the preceding vignette?

_____

_____

_____

_____

_____

_____

_____

_____

_____

What assumptions has Ms. Catelli made? What assumptions has Adrian made? How about Tom?

_____

_____

_____

_____

_____

_____

_____

If you were Ms. Catelli, how would you handle this situation? What would you do tomorrow?

_____

_____

_____

_____

_____

_____

_____

_____

Reflection

Reflecting on organizations in which you have been employed, describe an organizational policy or practice that illustrates cultural destructiveness.

_____

_____

_____

_____

_____

_____

Describe a behavior or value of yours or of someone you know that illustrates cultural destructiveness.

_____

_____

_____

_____

_____

_____

_____

◼ Cultural Incapacity

Cultural incapacity is any policy, practice, or behavior that venerates one culture over all others. In culturally incapacitating organizations, employees behave in ways that disempower people who differ from them culturally. In culturally incapacitating classrooms, the most frequent illustrations of disempowerment arise from holding low expectations for learners. These low expectations may be held by instructors, based on their perceptions of various cultural groups. Lowered expectations also result in tokenism.

Thus, disempowerment is an interactive phenomenon in which a dominant group renders another group powerless and the nondominant group perceives (and reinforces) its own powerlessness by internalizing its own oppression. Most of us are familiar with the actions of the dominant group; although we may view those actions with disdain, they are relatively easier to understand than the actions of the nondominant group. Paulo Freire (1987/1999) discusses this behavior of nondominant groups in his concept of internalized oppression. *Internalized oppression* occurs when members of an oppressed group take on the attitudes or worldview of their oppressor. They see themselves as inferior and often treat one another in the same demeaning way as their external oppressor has treated them.

⟵

Reflection

Carefully consider the following examples of *cultural incapacity*— lowered expectations or internalized oppression:

- Have you ever been aware of a female learner saying that she is not good in math because girls don't do well in math? Have you heard male learners make such a comment? Have you or your colleagues ever made such a statement? How did you react?

_____

_____

_____

_____

- Have you ever been reluctant to work with learners from a particular cultural group because of your perception that they are not good students? Have you heard this from colleagues? Have you heard it from other learners? Describe your reactions.

_____

_____

_____

_____

- Have you been aware of colleagues or other learners who ascribe stereotypic labels to learners because their primary language is other than English? Do you think they would respond in the same way if the accent was French or Danish? What if it was Arabic or Swahili? Why or why not?

_____

_____

_____

_____

- Have you heard colleagues or other learners excuse the low academic performance of learners in a nondominant group by pointing to the one person who is an outstanding example in that group? How did you react in this situation?

_____

_____

_____

_____

━━

Reflection

Create your own list of examples of lowered expectations and tokenism.

_____

_____

_____

_____

_____

_____

_____

Now, write your reactions to the information about cultural incapacity.

_____

_____

_____

_____

_____

_____

_____

━━

Add the following to the list of examples that you have developed:

Alicia Alvarez, the director of Training and Staff Develop-ment at the University Medical Center, is initiating a new program for aspiring managers. At this facility, the intern physi-cians tend to be males and females from the State University Medical Institute and from Asia and South America. Conversely, most of the managers are white males who have come from a prominent, private university known for its MBA program. The medical center has taken pride in its entry-level managers being sought after by hospitals throughout the country, which has added to the prestige of UMC. The board of directors, at its last meeting, decided that it had to be more proactive in recruiting members of underrepresented groups into management positions. They made it perfectly clear that this was not to be a closeted af-firmative action program and that they wanted all candidates to be fully qualified, both academically and experientially. Alicia has taken this new directive to heart in recruiting candidates into the Career Ladder Program (CLP). CLP is limited to 15 candidates annually, and the current class is the most diverse class ever, com-prising both women and men: 7 European American, 4 Asian Pacific, 2 African American, and 2 Central American cadidates.

"Welcome, everyone, to the orientation session!" Alicia exclaims. "This is such an exciting year. This is the most diverse class in the history of CLP. As you know, this movement toward diversity is a directive from the board."

"Excuse me, what do you mean by 'directive'?" Tanya queried.

"Isn't it obvious?" answered Paul. "I mean no disrespect, but don't you find it strange that for several years, people of color, or whatever you're called now, couldn't qualify and now suddenly we are overwhelmed by diversity?"

"Hey, why are you so hostile?" Katya jumped in. "We are going to be together weekly for 20 weeks, and you already have an attitude."

Alicia shouted, "Please, everyone! Maybe the word 'direc-tive' was a misstatement on my part."

"You can call it a misstatement if you want," Paul sniped, "but I think it is probably a slip of the truth."

⟶

Reflection

What are the issues of cultural incapacity in the vignette?

_____

_____

_____

_____

_____

What assumptions has Alicia made? What about Paul?

_____

_____

_____

_____

_____

What do you make of Katya's comment?

_____

_____

_____

_____

_____

If you were Alicia, how would you handle this situation differently? What would you do at the next meeting?

_____

_____

_____

_____

Think about organizations in which you have been employed, and describe an organizational policy or practice that reflects cultural incapacity.

_____

_____

_____

_____

Describe a behavior or value of yours or of someone you know that illustrates cultural incapacity.

_____

_____

_____

_____

▣ Cultural Blindness

Cultural blindness is any policy, practice, or behavior that ignores existing cultural differences or that considers such differences inconsequential. Often, people of goodwill speak proudly of "not seeing color, just seeing human beings." We find this stance the most vexing point on the continuum. People who hold cultural blindness as a value often fail to observe the effect they are having on others. For example, over the years we have recorded these comments from fellow educators:

In my classroom, I don't see color. I treat all students the same.

As superintendent, I take one day per week and visit classrooms throughout our school district. I have to tell you, after visiting any given classroom, I can't tell you the ethnic, racial, or gender composition of the classroom.

Most culturally blind instructors do not intend to harm others, or to benefit from the harm done to others. Nonetheless, from a systemic standpoint, most people from the dominant cultural group unwittingly and unintentionally benefit from the various forms of oppression that affect people from nondominant cultural groups. Moreover, when members of a dominant group value cultural blindness, they cause further unintended harm by contributing to the sense of invisibility experienced by members of nondominant groups. Often, people who value cultural blindness don't realize how their blindness leads to a sense of invisibility for those belonging to nondominant cultural groups.

Ironically, members of cultural groups who pride themselves on such cultural identifiers as skin color, hair styles, clothing styles, music, and dance may also contribute to other people's stereotypes of the individuals within those cultural groups. The culturally blind may believe the cultural differences are only visible cultural identifiers.

Another illusion that contributes to cultural blindness is the myth of the American melting pot. Such a mythical aim may have been desirable in the late 19th and early 20th centuries for some immigrants from eastern and southern Europe. However, it is neither desirable nor attainable for millions of Americans, now or in the past. These Americans have been the victims of legalized oppression, systematically denied access to the opportunities available to most other Americans.

Cultural invisibility and blindness comes in many, many forms:

The trainer of a conflict management class says, "I don't see color, I just see participants in my workshop."

An instructor takes a course in African American history in his graduate program with the intention of learning more about the accomplishments, trials, and tribulations of African Americans. None of the information repeats what he learned from his undergraduate major in U.S. history.

An administrator who takes a food-fun-and-fiestas or heroes-holidays-and-haute-cuisine approach to diversity declares, "Diversity is about celebrating what we have in common. All that other anger stuff just doesn't matter!"

A fifth-grade teacher says, "I really want to be fair to all my students, so I treat them all alike."

A college professor asks, "Why all the fuss about ethnic studies? In America, we have one history. Why not just focus on American history?"

In the preceding vignettes, the instructors have failed to note the difference between equity and equality. The inability to distinguish between these two fundamental concepts is characteristic of the culturally blind instructor. *Equality* refers to having identical privileges, status, or rights, regardless of the individual's needs, current situation, background, or context. *Equity* refers to being just, impartial, and fair, taking into consideration individual differences (Boyer, Ellis, Harris, & Soukhanov, 1983). For years, many police departments and fire departments had minimum height and weight requirements that they applied *equally* to all applicants. Because the average man differed from the average woman in terms of height and weight, these requirements were not *equitable* because they disproportionately barred more women than men from entering these departments. Instead, these departments now more *equitably* require that all their prospective employees pass minimum tests of physical strength, endurance, and flexibility that men and women can both work to achieve.

In an educational environment, the Scholastic Assessment Test (SAT) is designed so that all students are given the same test, under the same conditions, and with the same scoring policies. Hence, everyone has an equal chance of doing well on the SAT. Some students, however, are able to purchase specialized tutorials, coaching, and test preparation, whereas others are not able to buy additional aids in preparing for the test. In fact, many students may have outside factors that limit their ability to perform well (poor nutrition, lack of sleep, low expectations for doing well, increased environmental stress, inadequate school facilities or materials, etc.). For these reasons, students may not have an *equitable* chance of doing well on the SAT, despite the test designers' best intentions to provide an *equal* chance for every student to do well.

Instructors know that the learners who enter the classroom or training room come with different backgrounds and experiences. Effective instructors approach the classroom or training room assuming that each learner arrives with variations in knowledge, skills, and prior educational experiences. These instructors know the learners' educational needs and realize that school curricula usually fail to include multiple perspectives or experiences. Therefore, they strive for equity when addressing the learners' needs for learning new knowledge and skills, and they consider equality to be a worthy, if distant, goal for a future time, when equity has been achieved.

Activity

With your colleagues, discuss these examples of cultural blindness, then create a list of your own examples.

_____

_____

_____

_____

_____

_____

⟿

Helen Williams, a gifted and experienced preschool teacher at Maple View Elementary School, directs the school's English language learners (ELL) program. Helen is widely respected in the community and has been particularly effective in communicating with the parents of children who are English language learners. In her role as director, she visited the morning class and observed the new teacher, Bonnie Charlton. Bonnie is a first-year teacher who is working on completing the course work for her state teaching certification. She is entering teaching as a second career. She is enthusiastic about being a teacher and wants to do her very best. Bonnie has confided in Helen that she is concerned about teaching children who don't speak English fluently because she doesn't speak their language.

"Bonnie," said Helen, "please describe your classroom arrangement for me."

"Oh, yes, I am so excited about my plan," said Bonnie. "I decided to arrange the American kids and the migrant kids in different groups."

"Talk to me about your rationale," said Helen. "Do they stay separated the entire day?"

"Well, yes," Bonnie replied. "I just want to make sure the others do not hold the American kids back. Actually, this helps me do a better job with the migrant kids."

Helen continued to press, "We need to talk further with your grouping practices because I do have a major concern, but before we do so, I'm curious. It seems that you have a lot of girls named 'Maria.' "

"No, I don't," Bonnie replied. "I have only one girl named Maria. You know, I have never taken Spanish, and I find their names to be very hard to pronounce, so I decided to call each of the girls 'Maria' until I have a chance to learn their names."

Reflection

What are the issues of cultural blindness in this vignette?

What assumptions has Bonnie made?

_____

_____

_____

_____

_____

_____

_____

If you were Helen Williams, how would you handle this situation? What would you say next?

_____

_____

_____

_____

_____

_____

_____

_____

⟍⟋

Reflection

Describe your classroom experiences with behaviors or attitudes that reflect cultural blindness.

_____

_____

_____

_____

_____

_____

Reflecting on organizations in which you have been employed, describe an organizational policy or practice that illustrates cultural blindness.

_____

_____

_____

_____

_____

_____

_____

Describe a behavior or value of yours or of someone you know that illustrates cultural blindness.

_____

_____

_____

_____

_____

_____

_____

⟿

■ Cultural Precompetence

People and organizations that are *culturally precompetent* recognize that their skills and practices are limited when interacting with other cultural groups. They may have made some changes in their approaches to the issues arising from diversity, but they are aware that they need assistance and more information. The examples in the following vignettes are dilemmas encountered by a college instructor, a school district superintendent, and a community college administrator. The common denominator in each case is the realization that what they were doing was not working and that they were going to have to do something different.

A chemistry instructor at State University learned that many of his students were immigrants from Portugal. Even though he knew that most of them spoke English fluently, he also knew that they took great pride in their cultural heritage. This was a very new culture to him, even though he had taken a semester of Portuguese in addition to his three years of Spanish language in high school. In an attempt to establish rapport with the students, he decided to pronounce the word "Portuguese" with what he thought would be the appropriate accent. Unfortunately, his Portuguese had a poor Spanish accent, and what the students heard was a word that sounded a lot like an ethnic slur for Portuguese people.

⟿

The superintendent of the Maple View School District was known across the region for being in the forefront of innovations that benefited the education of learners in Maple View. He had taken note that in the previous five years, the number of learners who were not fluent in English had increased dramatically. This increase had presented challenges that they had begun to address during the preceding two years. First, these students were overrepresented in the lowest-ability classes, and their parents were beginning to press for reasons as to why these students were in these classes. Second, there were isolated fights between English-speaking and non-English-speaking students at the high school.

The superintendent was concerned that the image of the community was being tarnished when the media described the fistfights as race riots. He knew that many of the parents had invested a lot of money in their homes in the Pine Ridge community and that the schools were a key to keeping property values high. Though the number of incidents at Pine Hills High School remained low, he was quite aware of what had happened in high schools in nearby New Metropolis as populations shifted, and he wanted to prevent riots from igniting in his district. In an effort to keep the concerned parents at bay and to continue his reputation for being on the cutting edge of educational innovation, he decided to have an external group from a prominent consulting firm conduct a human relations audit of the community.

⟿

For several years, the Tri-Counties Community College had received funding from the federal government to provide technical support for training retired members of the military service for second careers. Because of the extremely high quality of the program, the placement rate exceeded 95%. However, the administrators and faculty working in the program were almost all white, whereas the clerical and technical-support personnel were almost all people of color. In the most recent audit, the granting agency said that there appeared to be serious communication problems between the supervisors and the clerical-technical staff. Although the auditors were silent on the issue of ethnicity in the two levels of program staff, they expressed deep concerns about the communication issues. They indicated in their final report that continued funding would be contingent on satisfactorily responding to these issues.

The governing board of the college suggested to the president that this problem warranted immediate attention. She assigned the matter to the vice president for human resources, Dr. Geraldo Diaz. Geraldo saw this as an opportunity to approach the issue on a more systemic level. He sent a request for proposals (RFP) to consultants who had successful track records in working with issues arising from diversity. The major criteria in the RFP were to provide services that addressed the immediate problems of communication and problem solving and thereby addressed the underlying issues.

Activity

Do you understand how each of the situations you just read reflects cultural precompetence? If not, talk about these vignettes with a few of your colleagues before proceeding to the next vignette.

_____

_____

_____

_____

_____

_____

The Maple View School District was in its first year of disaggregating student achievement data. Though this was part of a new statewide initiative, most of the school leaders, both administrators and leaders in the teacher's union, were not sure what to do with it. Dr. Barbara Campbell, the assistant superintendent for curriculum and staff development, convened a committee representing lead teachers and key administrators in the school district. Dr. Lee Kim distributed the fourth- and eighth-grade test scores on the nationally normed achievement test, to have a focal point for the discussion. As the charts were being passed around the room, these comments were made:

"Wow, look at these test scores for the lowest quintile of fourth graders. Notice that most of their parents did not even complete high school!"

"Yes, and I don't want to appear racist, but notice how many are kids from the East Side of Maple View."

"Well, we are doing a good job with the high achievers."

Barbara Campbell returned to her office, deflated. What she had intended as a session in how best to serve the needs of underachieving learners turned into a session in reinforcing stereotypes. At the next meeting, she took a different approach.

Barbara started by saying, "Since our last meeting, I have given a lot of thought to this assignment to look at these data. I think we pursued the wrong path with these charts. Today, I want us to look for trends and patterns in the data and to ask questions of clarification."

"I thought we noted important trends in our first meeting," said Joyce Smith.

"Yes," said Brad Clark, "I thought we clearly pointed out the inadequacies of the children from the East Side."

Hakim Moustafa was puzzled. "I left here last time thinking that if we were using these data to inform ourselves about how to better provide for these students, I didn't get it. Dr. Campbell, how do you see today's agenda being any more productive?"

Indira Negri was thoughtful. "You know, I just completed a class with Dr. Ruth Johnson at the State University, and she showed us the power in looking at these data. Dr. Campbell, do you think she would be a resource we could call on?"

⟵

Reflection

What issues of cultural precompetence are described in the vignette?

_____

_____

_____

_____

_____

_____

_____

_____

What are the assumptions made by Ms. Smith, Mr. Clark, and Mr. Moustafa? What assumptions are being made by Dr. Campbell and Ms. Negri?

_____

_____

_____

_____

_____

_____

_____

If you were Dr. Campbell, how would you handle this situation? What would you say to Ms. Negri?

_____

_____

_____

_____

_____

_____

_____

_____

Describe your classroom experiences with behaviors or attitudes that reflect cultural precompetence.

_____

_____

_____

_____

_____

_____

_____

Reflecting on organizations in which you have been employed, describe an organizational policy or practice that illustrates cultural precompetence.

_____

_____

_____

_____

_____

_____

_____

_____

Describe a behavior or value of yours or of someone you know that illustrates cultural precompetence.

_____

_____

_____

_____

_____

_____

_____

⟿

◼ Cultural Competence

Cultural competence is any policy, practice, or behavior that uses the essential elements of cultural proficiency as the standard for the individual or the organization. As you may recall, these essential elements are assessing culture, valuing diversity, managing the dynamics of difference, adapting to diversity, and institutionalizing cultural knowledge. Though these elements are presented here and in the chapters that follow as separate concepts, in practice, they function interactively.

Culturally competent instructors or organizations are students of themselves and of their organizations, either because they purposely set out to study themselves and their organizations or because their personal ethical framework involves their continual observation of themselves and their organizations in seeking to do what they believe is best. These instructors realize that all learners have the capacity to learn and that it is the instructor's responsibility to create an environment in which the learner can use that capacity for learning. In contrast to the vignette with Dr. Campbell and the precompetent committee, the culturally competent committee would have used the data to ask this key question: What is it that we have to do differently for these children and youths to succeed academically and socially?

R ose Diaz-Harris, the assistant principal at Maple View Middle School, also demonstrated effective use of the essential elements. The school had recently undergone review by its regional accrediting agency (RAA). A team of 15 educators spent five days on campus studying the school from every conceivable angle. Their primary documents were the school's self-study responding to the RAA's standards for excellence and many other documents at the school site. In addition, the team made classroom observations and conducted extensive interviews with faculty and staff members, students, community members, parents, and all major advisory and decision-making groups. At the end of their visit, they issued a comprehensive report that, though generally positive, included the disturbing finding that participation in the school's extracurricular activities did not reveal an equitable participation by the various ethnic groups that attended the school.

Rose was given the task of collecting and disaggregating the data, analyzing it, and making appropriate recommendations. She developed a two-pronged strategy. First, she collected the data from the school's data system and disaggregated it by gender and ethnicity. The patterns she found could only be identified as segregated. In interviewing learners, she found that the activities were identified as intended for European American students, African American students, Latino students, or Asian Pacific students. Only the student government and the major sports teams were integrated in a fashion that represented the profile of the school.

Second, Rose and a group of instructors used the essential elements to develop a strategic plan for improving student involvement in the school's extracurricular program. Their overarching goal for the next academic year was to involve sports and activity sponsors in recruiting students from across the campus into the activities. The school faculty decided that the extracurricular program exists to provide students with successful social experiences as an important adjunct to the curricular program of the school. The school administration and faculty now view both the curricular and the extracurricular programs as fundamental to student success. A major part of that success is providing students with the opportunity to develop cross-cultural relationships.

Once the school administrators and faculty members had agreed about their major goals, Rose formed a committee comprising activity sponsors, coaches, and students to review the disaggregated data in light of the goals. Rose made a short presentation on the essential elements of cultural competence and opened the floor to questions and comments.

Coach Kao said, "You know, I had noticed that my tennis team was mostly white and Asian students, of course, but I had not viewed it as exclusionary. I can see where that would be a possible view."

Lucy Simmons responded, "I could not agree more. That is the case with the chess club, too. It had not occurred to me that we don't go out and recruit students who are willing to learn chess. Basically, what we do is organize tournaments within members of the club."

"I think what we are talking about has a lot of importance," said Tom Lee. "Frequently, I sense tension among racial groups of students on campus. As the student body president, it seems to me that using the extracurricular activities as a means of outreach could be a good step in promoting harmony on campus. It is like in our classes; some teachers provide opportunities for us to work in groups, but most do not. There is a sense of isolation on campus."

"Though I am the activity adviser," Lou Bono said, "I want to speak as an instructor at this school. I think Rose is onto something here. Ever since the incident at Columbine High School, two things have haunted me. First is the obvious concern for those who were shot. However, the message that stays with me was the statement by the principal on the opening day of school the next fall. You may have seen it on CNN. I recall that he said to the assembled students, faculty, and staff that it was their collective responsibility to involve the students on the edge of the school's culture in the life of the school. If that is not a telling comment, I don't know what is. Not that I think that would necessarily happen here, but just to acknowledge that there are students 'on the edge of the culture' is pretty revealing. I bet that would describe the situation in nearly every school in the country."

Reflection

What are the issues of cultural competence presented in the vignette?

_____

_____

_____

_____

_____

_____

_____

_____

_____

_____

What assumptions are made by Coach Kao, Lucy Simmons, Tom Lee, and Lou Bono?

_____

_____

_____

_____

_____

_____

_____

_____

If you were Rose, how would you proceed?

_____

_____

_____

_____

_____

_____

_____

_____

⟿

Reflection

Describe your experiences as an instructor with behaviors or attitudes that reflect cultural competence.

_____

_____

_____

_____

_____

_____

Reflecting on organizations in which you have been employed, describe an organizational policy or practice that illustrates cultural competence.

_____

_____

_____

_____

_____

_____

_____

Describe a behavior or value of yours or of someone you know that illustrates cultural competence.

____

____

____

____

____

____

____

____

Cultural Proficiency

Cultural proficiency is manifest in organizations and people who esteem culture, who know how to learn about individual and organizational cultures, and who interact effectively with a variety of cultural groups. Cultural proficiency is not a destination but, rather, a way of being. It is an ongoing and unfolding process as you learn about yourself, your organization, and the people who work with you.

At the University Medical Center, Charles Sisson, the manager of the public health team, was frustrated. He had organized African American and Spanish-speaking teams to reach out to prospective African American and Hispanic clients. The Spanish-speaking team was doing very well and exceeding their quota of new patients who sought health care information at the walk-in clinic. The African American workers were not doing so well, so he had some of those team members come back to the office to help with paperwork and filing.

This action was not received well at all. He couldn't understand why the African American workers were giving him so much attitude, so he called Alicia Alvarez, the director of Training and Staff Development, to talk with his people.

"Charles is underestimating us," LaTanya complained. "Doesn't he get that cultural proficiency stuff? We all had to go to the workshops. You should have made him go, too, because we want to do this work in a culturally competent way, and he doesn't get it."

"First of all," said Joey, "Charles insists that we approach all the prospects the same way. That is just stupid. Our prospective African American clients access the health care system differently than the Hispanic clients—and will you tell him to stop referring to them as 'Spanish'? Many of the Hispanic prospects are first- or second-generation, so they have a different attitude toward authority and wellness. Our approach to African Americans has to be different so that we can earn their trust and get them into the clinics."

"Trying to treat each client group equally is undermining our success. We need to have strategies that suggest we understand our clients."

"But that is only part of the problem," LaTanya continued. "Charles has the staff segregated. Now he's right, we can't all speak Spanish, but we could learn. Why doesn't he give us a chance? Let us take some Spanish classes. Let us work as integrated teams so that we can learn from one another."

Culturally proficient instructors don't know everything there is to know, but they probably know what they need to know, and they know how to ask for help.

⟁

Reflection

Reflecting on organizations in which you have been employed, describe an organizational policy or practice that illustrates cultural proficiency.

_____

_____

_____

Describe a behavior or value of yours or of someone you know that illustrates cultural proficiency.

⟿

Chart 5.1 gives brief descriptions of the phases of the cultural-proficiency continuum, along with examples to illustrate each phase.

CHART 5.1   *The Six Phases Along the Cultural Proficiency Continuum*

Cultural destructiveness: The elimination of another cultural group or the suppression of the culture's practices

Cultural incapacity: Treatment of members of nondominant groups based on stereotypes and with the belief that the dominant group is inherently superior

Cultural blindness: Failure to see or to acknowledge that differences between groups often make a difference to the groups and to the individuals who are members of those groups

Cultural precompetence: Behavior or practices that seek to acknowledge cultural differences in healthy ways but that are not quite effective

Cultural competence: Effective interactions with individuals and groups of people from different ethnic and social cultures; use of the essential elements as the standards for individual behavior and organizational practice

Cultural proficiency: Practices that reflect knowing how to learn and teach about different groups; having the capacity to teach and to learn about differences in ways that acknowledge and honor all people and the groups they represent

Reflection

Going Deeper

Think about your classroom and about other classrooms in which you've observed, perhaps as a learner. List a teaching practice or behavior (or an organizational policy or practice) that illustrates each of the six phases along the continuum.

Cultural destructiveness

_____

_____

_____

_____

Cultural incapacity

_____

_____

_____

_____

Cultural blindness

_____

_____

_____

_____

Cultural precompetence

_____

_____

_____

_____

Cultural competence

_____

_____

_____

_____

Cultural proficiency

_____

_____

_____

_____

⟿

Part II

Essential Elements of Cultural Proficiency

Essential Elements of the Culturally Proficient Instructor

As a culturally proficient instructor, you will do the following:

1. **Assess culture.** You'll be aware of your own culture and the effect it may have on the people in your classroom. You'll learn about the culture of the organization and the cultures of the learners, and you'll anticipate how they will interact with conflict with, and enhance one another.

2. **Value diversity.** You'll welcome a diverse group of learners into your classroom and appreciate the challenges diversity brings. You'll share this appreciation with the learners in your class, developing a community of learning with them.

3. **Manage the dynamics of difference.** You'll recognize that conflict is a normal and natural part of life. You'll develop skills to manage conflict in a positive way. You'll also help the learners to understand that what appear to be clashes in personalities may in fact be conflicts in culture.

4. **Adapt to diversity.** You'll commit to continuously learning what is necessary to deal with the issues caused by differences. You'll enhance the substance and structure of the courses you teach so that all instruction is informed by the guiding principles of cultural proficiency.

5. **Institutionalize cultural knowledge.** You'll work to influence the culture of your organization so that its policies and practices are informed by the guiding principles of cultural proficiency. You'll also take advantage of teachable moments to share cultural knowledge about the instructors, their managers, the learners, and the communities from which they come. You'll create opportunities for these groups to learn about one another and to engage in ways that honor who they are and challenge them to be better still.

6

Assessing
Your Culture

Naming the Differences

*How do I describe my culture? Don't you
have to be from somewhere else to really
have a culture?*

Over the past couple of decades, educators and other researchers
have written a great deal about learning styles. Thanks to the work
of Howard Gardner and others, instructors today, more than ever
before in the history of American education, have an opportunity to
know a great deal about how individual learners learn best. The literature clearly shows that no two learners, or groups of learners, process
information in the same way, nor do they read, hear, speak, or think in
the same way.

The obvious task for instructors is to find out how their students
learn best. This task is neither simple nor easy. The process of finding out
is called *assessment*.

The learners who enter your classroom have not only their own
learning styles but also their own distinctive cultural backgrounds and
experiences. As the person in charge of your students' learning, you also
bring to the classroom your own distinctive experiences and culture. As
a culturally proficient instructor, you understand, appreciate, and
respect the various cultures represented in your classroom, and you try
to proactively design instructional strategies that include all learners.
You also understand the power you possess by virtue of being the
instructor, the person *in charge*. How do you approach instruction and
learning in your classroom?

⟵

Getting Centered

What do you know about your own learning style? What do you know about how your own cultural background and experiences affects your learning? Under what conditions do you learn best? How do you respond as a learner when you are asked to do the same task, in the same way, within the same time period, using the same materials as other members of the group? Has an instructor ever asked you to describe the best way to teach you? Who is responsible for your learning—you or the instructor?

_____

_____

_____

_____

_____

_____

⟵

Learning Styles and Culturally Proficient Instruction

Culturally proficient instructors are aware of their own learning styles and the learning styles of their students. They also know about their own culture and the effects their culture may have on the other people in the classroom. They realize that instructors play a powerful role in the classroom.

When an instructor walks into the classroom for the first time with a new group or class, she or he is the center of attention. The learners look to see the physical attributes of the instructor: hair color, height, weight, and complexion. They wait to hear the sound of the instructor's voice and the first words spoken. The clothing the instructor wears, accessories and adornments, and the way the instructor looks at them—or doesn't look at them—intrigues the learners. The interaction between learner and instructor begins the moment the instructor enters the room, even before the learners ask the first question or engage in conversation.

D r. Barbara Campbell, the assistant superintendent for curriculum and staff development, was pleased to be giving the opening comments for the teachers' back-to-school inservice and picnic. She knew that several new instructors would be in the audience, and she wanted to make sure that they, as well as the returning teachers and staff members, would leave the opening session having a clear understanding of cultural proficiency and of the essential elements of culturally proficient instruction. After her presentation, she asked her colleague Nancy to review her speech and give her feedback.

"The speech was really good," Nancy said. "I like how you spelled out the importance of our teachers taking time to get to know each and every learner. But I was just wondering why you felt it was necessary to tell the audience about your own family reunion last summer. The part about your sister being a doctor and the two of you being raised by your grandmother, seems a little 'extra' to me. Is that part of the 'black experience' your people talk about?"

"It is about my experience, and I am black. So by sharing my own story and my family values, instructors may see how important it is to share their cultural and family values with their learners. I hope that what I say will model the inside-out perspective of cultural proficiency. We get to know our learners one student at a time, you know. By the way, didn't you recently visit your sister back East? Let's go get a cup of coffee. I want to hear all about this favorite sister of yours."

The culturally proficient instructor understands the powerful effect of culture on what takes place in the classroom. Knowing your own culture and how others interact with you is critical to culturally proficient instruction. Cultural proficiency's inside-out approach to diversity encourages instructors to understand and acknowledge their own cultures. That is, the essential element "assessing culture" begins with the individual or the organization first assessing her or his or its own culture. With this self-assessment comes a greater appreciation of how diverse learners interact with you the instructor.

R alph, an eighth-grade teacher, was preparing for his first
day in his own classroom at Pine View Middle School. The
bulletin boards were ready. The class roster was complete. Textbooks were on the shelves. Ralph walked down the hallway to ask
his mentor teacher, Charlene Brennaman, one final question:
"Charlene, how will I know how to teach them?"
"Teach them the way they learn best."
"How will I know how they learn best?"
"Ask them. They will tell you, and they will show you how to
teach them. All you have to do is ask." Then, she paused, turned
back to him once more, and added, "and ask often."

So how do you become aware of and knowledgeable about how the
learners in your classroom learn best? A starting point is for you to know
how you, yourself, learn best. As an adult learner, you probably have not
been asked recently to think about your own learning. Intuitively, many
of us go about our routines of reading, writing, speaking, and listening in
ways that are most comfortable to us.

Think of the conflict—or the comedy—that might erupt if parents
and children sat down at the breakfast table and took turns reading the
morning newspaper aloud—followed by a brief quiz on the content.
Funny as it may seem, isn't that what instructors sometimes ask classrooms of 30 learners to do? Isn't the process similar when a personnel
director hands out a procedures manual to 14 new employees and says,
"Take 10 minutes and silently read pages 2 through 7, then I'll give you a
quiz to see whether you know the correct procedures"?

At the breakfast table, many parents encourage each person to choose
a section of the newspaper to read silently—or they encourage discussion
of issues more personal to each family member. An alternative for the personnel director might be to allow each of the new employees time to read,
ask questions, and think about the assigned section in the procedures
manual before administering the quiz. Instead, the director might ask the
employees to perform the required task rather than to write about it. These
strategies create a safer, less threatening learning environment and take
into consideration students' differences in learning styles.

Becoming Aware of Each Learner's Uniqueness

Imagine for a moment that you are standing on the shoreline of an Alas-
kan city looking out over the vast inland waterway filled with massive

icebergs. Each iceberg floats independently, but the collection of the icebergs offers an even more impressive scene. As you stand in awe of the
magnificence of the iceberg field, a friend standing nearby offers you a
pair of special binoculars so that you can actually see below the surface
of the water. You are a bit skeptical, at first, but you trust your friend's
innovative ideas, so you take the special binoculars and hold them to
your eyes. To your amazement, you can now see what you only sus-
pected moments before. Below the surface is the gigantic outline of one
of the icebergs. It plunges deep below the surface and has features unlike
the ice that protrudes above the surface. You can see the detail of the ice
formation and the texture and hues that you could not see when your
view was confined to the surface. Then, still looking through the binoculars, you notice something even more profound. Each iceberg is unique.
Some have sharp, craggy edges; others appear smoother, almost
glasslike. As many icebergs as there are floating in the waterway, there
are as many different appearances to the shapes and sizes of each iceberg. Each one is unique in its own design.

Reluctantly, you return the special glasses to your friend. You are
somewhat sad because you would like to keep the glasses so you could
always see the uniqueness of the icebergs. Your friend takes the glasses
and says, "Now that you have seen below the surface, you'll never look
at them the same way again. You won't need the special glasses anymore. You are special because of what you see now."

Just as you were able to see the unique aspects of icebergs even after
removing your special glasses, you will be able to see the unique aspects
of your learners even after you finish reading this book on cultural proficiency. Once you have learned how to be sensitive to your students' distinctive cultural backgrounds, experiences, and learning styles, you will
be able to view them this way without the aid of your "special glasses."
The essential elements of cultural proficiency will serve as your special
glasses for recognizing each student's unique individuality and distinctive cultural background. Each classroom of learners will present you
with a new opportunity to see each learner's uniqueness. Your special
sensitivity will enhance your instruction and facilitate your students'
learning. Your knowledge of cultures and of learning styles will help you
and the learners in the complex cognitive process of learning.

In addition to gaining understanding of your students' cultures, you
will enhance your instruction by assessing your own culture and the
organizational culture in which you work and teach. As a culturally proficient instructor, you will assess the impact of your own culture on your
instructional behaviors. You will see that your preferences for instructional strategies may be grounded in your own learning style rather than

in the style best suited to your learners. As a culturally proficient instructor, you will know and appreciate the complexity and importance of the diverse cultures in your classroom or training program. You will realize the impact of your own attitudes, habits, feelings, and actions on your students or trainees. You will also demonstrate a variety of instructional strategies that respect and support the various cultures of the learners you teach.

Reflection

Do you recall an experience when the learners reacted negatively to you as an instructor? Were they reacting to you as a person, to the lesson itself, or to the situational context of the learning? What did you do in response to the negative behavior? If you answered no to the first question here, do you know why learners have always reacted to you in a positive way? Who are the learners? Who are you in the presence of the learners? What difference does your approach make in how learners respond to you?

_____

_____

_____

_____

_____

_____

Assessing Your Culture

Culturally proficient instructors are aware of their own culture. As a culturally proficient instructor, you are also aware that your culture acts on and through your instructional behaviors in the classroom. A brief self-assessment using the following questions can guide you to a deeper understanding of the relationship between knowing your culture and choosing appropriate instructional strategies.

⟶

DO THIS Reflection

Activity

What do you know about your own name? How does it reflect your cultural heritage? How does your name reflect your family's history? How does it reflect your personal history?

_____

_____

_____

_____

_____

_____

How do others respond when they read or hear your name in your presence?

_____

_____

_____

_____

_____

_____

Have you thought about your entrance into the classroom of new learners? What happens when you walk into the classroom for the first time? Have you ever noticed how the learners respond?

_____

_____

_____

_____

_____

How do you describe your culture?

_____

_____

_____

_____

_____

Do you wait to describe your culture until a member of the class asks you about it, or do you share aspects of your culture as part of the classroom instruction?

_____

_____

_____

_____

_____

In addition to instructional time, what opportunities do you have to share with your students some information about your culture?

_____

_____

_____

_____

_____

Have you noticed that learners of your culture react and relate to you in different ways than do learners from cultures that differ from yours?

_____

_____

_____

_____

⟿

Reflection

How did you respond to each of the questions in the preceding assessment? Who are you? What do you want others to know about you as a person, an instructor, and a learner? Take a few minutes to write our own story.

_____

_____

_____

_____

⟞

In addition to assessing your own culture, you will be involved in helping others to assess their own cultures. In the following vignette, the instructor fails to elicit the responses she seeks from her trainees. As you read the vignette, think about how you might have handled the situation differently.

Cynthia, the training officer at Community National Bank (CNB), is beginning the first day of diversity training for all bank employees. She has asked the group to respond to a question during an icebreaker activity: "Introduce yourself by giving your name, your cultural background, and any specialized training that you have had."

Harland, one of the participants, protests, "I'm American. I don't have a culture like you do. What am I supposed to say? How do I describe my culture, except to say that I am white and I'm American? Don't you have to be from somewhere else, a person of color to really have a culture?"

Neither the trainer nor the other participants were aware of the impact Cynthia's question would have on different members of the group. Harland responded defensively, assuming that because the training was about diversity, the question was intended for people of color, thereby excluding white people from having "culture." Cynthia, however, had hoped the question would allow each person in the group to describe her or his cultural background, regardless of ethnicity. She had also hoped that knowing the culture of others would help the members of the group respect and appreciate each other.

The instructor in the preceding vignette had assumed that all the people in the group knew their cultural backgrounds and would be willing to openly share that information. She also assumed that everyone already agreed with one of her deeply held beliefs: Acknowledging our cultural differences and similarities is an effective way for a group of employees to work and learn together. By failing to realize that the trainees did not all share her belief at the start of the training, she prompted stronger resistance to the training she wanted to offer.

Reflection

Put yourself in the role of Cynthia at the CNB diversity training. What would you have done differently? Possibly, a more culturally proficient approach in the situation at the bank would have been for Cynthia to give the following instructions for the opening activity:

"Culture is everything you believe and do that identifies you as a part of a group and distinguishes you from other groups. Most people think of culture as their race or ethnicity, but we are much more complex than that. Most people belong to several groups and identify strongly with two or three. So when I ask you to talk about your culture, I am asking you to think about the groups you identify with or from which you derive your identity. I'd like each of you to tell a little about your cultural background. Perhaps you'd like to start with your name.

"Probably one of the most treasured possessions that we have is our name. Think of your own name and what it means to you and your family. Share with one other person in the room what your name is, what your name means, how your name was chosen, or any interesting story or information about your name. After about five minutes for each of you to talk about your own name, I will ask that you introduce your partner to the rest of the group. You tell your partner's story."

What is your reaction to the preceding introductory comments? Write and rehearse your own script, describing the purpose of knowing one's own culture, as well as the culture of the learners.

_____

_____

_____

_____

_____

_____

_____

⤙

Assessing Organizational Culture

Thus far, we have noted that culturally proficient instructors assess their own culture, come to understand their students' cultures, and help their students assess their own cultures. In addition, they assess the organizational culture of the environments in which they teach. Organizations have cultures, and each member of the organization functions within the organizational culture. To be effective and successful within an organization, you must assess its organizational culture and learn how to behave appropriately within it. This assessment and awareness of organizational culture helps you to know what behaviors are expected and affirmed within the organization.

⤙

Reflection

Think of a time when you violated one of the unwritten rules of your school or company. How did you know you had broken the rule? How were you expected to have known the rule? How do you learn the cultural expectations of an organization?

_____

_____

_____

_____

_____

_____

_____

By knowing about and understanding the culture of the organization in which you work, you will be better able to interact with learners, confront and conflict with colleagues, and enhance your organizational relationships and communication. As a culturally proficient instructor, you will work toward establishing the cultural norms within your organization. You will help to determine those norms after assessing the values and beliefs held by members of the organization. You will recognize that these norms must reflect working agreements shared by the organizations' members. Once these cultural norms are established, you will ensure that they are stated explicitly and shared by leaders and workers throughout the organization.

It is important for members of the organization to know and assess how others—both inside and outside the organization—perceive the organization. Most people learn an organization's culture intuitively. When you are working with a diverse group of people, they may not have the cultural background to intuit the cultural norms of your particular organization. A culturally proficient instructor articulates the organization's cultural expectations to all learners. At times, it may be useful to evaluate your organizational culture by using an assessment instrument as a tool to analyze and understand the impact of this culture on instruction and learning. The results of the assessment can then guide you in adjusting your presentation style, in selecting materials, and in determining your instructional strategies.

Carlos Montanaro, owner and operator of the Maple View Rock and Cement Company, meets with all new employees to give them a tour of the company on their first day on the job. He gives each new employee a company logo lapel pin and starts the tour by looking at photos of his father and the first employees when the company began, 25 years ago. Today, he is meeting and greeting new employee Rick Barnard, a truck driver.

"I am pleased and proud to welcome you to our company," Carlos begins. "We are a family here. This business is my family's business. As you can see in these pictures, my father was a hard-working man who worked right along with the employees. I do the same thing. You will see me in the yard or driving a truck or loading an order or working on the books here in the office. I will always be where the work and the workers are."

"Thanks for spending this time with me, Mr. Montanaro," said Rick. "I heard what a good company this is and what a great guy you are to work for. I'm glad to be here. I do have a few questions, though. I also heard that you help folks get started again with their education or training. I had to drop out of community college to make a living for my family. What chance do I have here to get some more training? And one more thing, I don't speak Spanish or any other foreign language. Is that a problem? I noticed that a lot of the guys here do speak Spanish."

"Come with me," Carlos answered, "and I'll introduce you to a few of the employees who are going back to school or have completed a new training program since they came to work with us. They can tell you how things really are around here. Then, you come back to me at the end of the day and tell me what you heard from everyone you meet today. And about being Spanish-speaking, we appreciate our workers here for what they know and what they are willing to learn. Just ask for help when you need it. Welcome to Maple View Rock and Cement Company and welcome to the family."

⟶

Reflection

Think about the organization in which you work. Is the organization as a whole supportive of instruction and learning? Do members of the organization affirm and value employees from diverse cultures?

_____

_____

_____

_____

_____

_____

_____

Think of a time when you were a member of a planning team for an employee workshop or training session. What role did your culture or ethnicity play in the planning process? Were cultural differences topics of discussion in the planning sessions? Did the planning team make efforts to respect and allow for cultural differences of the trainers and the learners? How did the conversation about individual differences sound to you? As a culturally proficient instructor, how could you frame the next planning session to include norms for cultural proficiency?

_____

_____

_____

_____

_____

_____

_____

As mentioned previously, it is important for instructors to know and assess how others, both inside and outside the organization, perceive the organization. Those outside the organization behave in ways that are consistent with their perceptions of how the organization treats its employees, its learners, and its community. Often, members of a community will avoid calling the school or coming to the school if they have heard that the teachers don't value parent involvement. Community members avoid working with certain agencies when they perceive that the agency does not value diversity. When the employees of an organization treat people outside the organization in ways that are demeaning and disrespectful, the outside community views the organization itself in the same way. By assessing this perception, the culturally proficient instructor is better able to understand why members of the learning community react negatively to members of the organization.

Carlos Montanaro's wife, Anita, is president of the Pine Hills High School PTA. Members of the community often ask her and Carlos questions about the high school. Both Carlos and Anita are very active in community and volunteer organizations throughout the city and have served on the city's leadership committee.

At a leadership committee meeting, Lupe, a member of the committee, asked Anita about some of the after-school programs at the high school: "Anita, I have been meaning to ask you about the after-school tutoring at the high school. Does your son Tony go to any of the sessions? We want Roberto to go, but he says he is not eligible to stay after school because he has to ride the bus home. What should I do to get him some help?"

"Oh, I think the school has an activity bus that takes kids home after the tutoring classes. Just call the school, and ask someone there to give you the information."

"I don't like to call the school," Lupe confessed. "My English is not very good, and I don't think they like it when I call. I always feel like I am causing them too much trouble. Besides, the activity bus only drops kids off on the West Side. They said it was too far and too many kids to drop off on the East Side where we live."

Anita sympathized, "I'm sorry you have not been well received at the school, Lupe. I'll mention your concerns to the school principal and to the PTA leadership council. We should all be working on these issues together."

Going Deeper

What have you learned from the vignettes in this chapter? What have you learned about yourself? What have you learned about the organization in which you work? Observe yourself over the next few weeks: How and what do you share about your values and your beliefs with the people you teach? What do you do to learn about the people in your classroom? How does that inform and influence what and how you teach?

_____

_____

_____

_____

_____

_____

_____

_____

_____

_____

_____

_____

_____

_____

NOTES

7

Valuing Diversity

Claiming the Differences

As a culturally proficient instructor, you open the minds and hearts of your learners, affirming that differences are not deficits.

Valuing is something we do naturally. You express your values all the time. All people do. As an instructor, you value learning. You decided to be an instructor because you value learning. You picked up this book because you were interested in the topic, and you have continued to read this book because you value what you are reading.

Getting Centered

Think of your closest friends. List their names on paper, or close your eyes and imagine them. Now think about what it is that you like about them. What do they have in common that you like? What are the unique characteristics they possess? As you think about their characteristics, what does this tell you about what you value in friendships?

_____

_____

_____

⚊

Each of us finds valued similarities among our friends—such as their intelligence, sense of humor, compassion, or sense of adventure. Among our friends we also find differences that we also value. One friend collects and repairs vintage automobiles. In her, you value how she focuses on an avocation. Another friend is confident in speaking out on social issues. In him, you value his commitment to his ideals. You may, or may not, invite all these people to the same dinner party, but they are your close friends just the same. The key element for you is that you value your friendships with these people, with their similarities and their differences. You value their diversity.

Diversity is as ever-present as the air we breathe. To ask, "Do you believe in diversity?" is tantamount to asking, "Do you believe in the sun?" Diversity is not something to believe in. It exists. We can look around us and see diversity everywhere we turn.

What creates a conflict for some is the need to say, "Yes I see diversity, but shouldn't we emphasize our similarities?" As the authors of this book, we respond, "Not necessarily. It is important to recognize the differences and to notice the differences that make a difference. Only then is it effective for an instructor to focus on similarities."

If you focused solely on similarities when you were teaching, you would be focusing only on the lowest common denominator among your learners. Just as you value the similarities and differences in your friends, you can appreciate that difference and similarity balance each other—the *yin* and *yang* of human existence. As a culturally proficient instructor, you look among the learners in your classroom and see both their similarities and their differences. You note the similarities and notice also the differences that make a difference.

Reflection

What is the nature of the diversity in your current professional setting? How would you describe it to someone who is visiting your classroom setting?

_____

_____

_____

_____

_____

_____

_____

Valuing Diversity Is an Intentional Act

In this book, we often use the term *intentionality,* which refers to the *principle of intentionality:* When you proceed with the conscious intention of doing something differently, you increase the likelihood of achieving your desired outcome. To act with intention is to behave with clear awareness of your goals and intentions and to keep those intentions in your consciousness as you go about your work. For example, if you intend to be a culturally proficient instructor, you may think about some particular changes in attitude and behavior that you want to focus on right now. Each time you walk into your classroom or training room, you remind yourself of your intention to be culturally proficient. Then, you pay careful attention to the specific behaviors that you are focusing on today.

To value diversity is to teach with the intention of valuing diversity and to pay attention to those things that reflect diversity in your classroom. As *good summary*

Vision . Mission Statement

Not true for ICS

True

an instructor who values diversity, you foster a learning community, recognizing that diversity is always present in your classroom, even when such diversity is not strongly evident. You organize your classroom so that materials, instructional delivery systems, and patterns of attention to learners fully acknowledge diversity. You value the diverse classroom as an opportunity to enhance your teaching and learning. You motivate students to learn, and you encourage learners to engage in the content, learn from one another, and develop healthy attitudes about society. You are informed by your teaching, continually learning and applying new strategies for learning. When viewed as a whole, your behaviors illustrate that you value diversity, revealing your commitment to the learning community. In valuing diversity, you see opportunities to learn from your students and your colleagues.

To value diversity is to be clear about what you and your organization value as important. Over the past decade or two, most organizations have engaged in creating vision and mission statements. It is nearly impossible to enter an organization today—school or corporate office—and not encounter its mission, vision, or core values statement. These statements almost always describe a value for diversity within the organization and in the community it serves. Such statements have meaning when they truly reflect the core values of the organization and the shared values of the people within it.

In reality, however, these statements are often written by small committees to satisfy an external accreditation agency and thus do not reflect how employees or constituent groups are valued or treated. For that reason, we believe that we must also observe a person's behavior or an organization's practices in order to determine the values of the person or organization. In our view, we show our values in what we say *and do.* When practices and stated values are incongruent, there is the potential for disconnection. In personal and organizational relationships, this leads to dysfunction. When they are congruent, and harmony prevails among the needs of the organization, its employees, and its constituent groups, we find productive people and organizations.

⟶

Reflection

Read the following questions, one at a time, then think; don't write, just think about your response. Then, go to the next question until you have read them all.

- Have you ever been in a situation in which a new employee entered your organization and you wondered whether she or he was an affirmative action hire?

- Have you been in a situation in which you wondered whether a person who spoke slowly and deliberately was very intelligent?

- Have you ever been in a setting in which one person spoke limited English and those around her or him spoke more loudly so the person could understand?

- Have you ever been in a situation in which you felt uncomfortable because you were noticeably different from others in the group?

- Does your organization honor some holidays but not yours?

- Does your organization have a mission statement that includes reaching out into the varied constituent communities it serves but, as a practical matter, serves one primary community?

Now, record your reactions to the questions. Don't answer the questions, just focus on how you felt as you read the questions. Your response will aid you in continuing to clarify your understanding of what it means to value diversity.

In each of the foregoing situations, an organization or the people in it apparently do not value difference. In these settings, difference was considered but not valued. Difference was tolerated, not valued. Sometimes, the first step toward valuing diversity is mere tolerance for differences. Also, sometimes tolerance is a decided improvement over culturally destructive reactions and interactions. Tolerance is often the first in a progression of steps that may lead to valuing diversity.

Culturally proficient instructors use specific diversity-valuing behaviors in the classroom and with colleagues. For one thing, they frame the conversation about learners around the differences that make a difference, and they pay attention to how to provide an effective learning environment for their diverse learners.

M aple View Elementary School is in the first year of a three-year educational reform process. Following directives from the state and guidance from the school district, the school has been examining disaggregated test data to inform the reform process. The state's department of education disaggregated reading, mathematics, and writing data from a widely used norm-referenced test in order for educators and community members to examine the subpopulations within each school.

Based on these test data, educators have concluded that children from low-income families are not performing nearly as well as they should. This is disproportionately the case for students who are African American, Latino, Native American, and Southeast Asian. Maple View Elementary School has formed an Educator-Parent-Business Community Team (EPBCT) to guide the development of an improvement plan. The EPBCT has conducted input sessions with parents and other members of the community, as well as with teachers and counselors, to gauge their perceptions of what is working well in the school and of what improvements are needed. The input sessions focused on curricular issues (e.g., reading, mathematics, and English language learning) and school climate issues (e.g., safety, the role of parents, and perceptions of the school). Those data have been studied, categorized, and readied for alignment with test scores.

At this evening's meeting, the test data are being distributed for the first time. The 12 members of the EPBCT are in attendance, and the facilitator from the district office is distributing the data. The data sheets summarize reading, mathematics, and writing results for the previous year's second-, fourth-, and sixth-grade students. The data are summarized by grade level and are disaggregated by gender and ethnicity. The data are then further disaggregated into five quintiles (i.e., each band of 20% of students: 1-20%; 21-40%, etc.). Accompanying the data sheets are demographic profiles of the families of students at the school. A profile of parents' ethnicity and of the number of years the students attended school is included. As the data sheets were being distributed, Karl said, "Wow! This is a ton of data. How will we ever make sense of this?"

"I don't know," Helen Williams replied, "but I am sure our facilitator will guide us as well as she did with the data from the input sessions."

Helen then heard one parent, Carolyn, comment to another, "Gosh, look at the levels of school completion by our parents! Nearly 62% of our parents have not gone beyond eighth grade. No wonder these test scores are so low!"

"You know," Helen said gently to Carolyn, "I hope we don't build obstacles for our children. It is our responsibility as educators to work with all children to attain high achievement levels."

The facilitator then addressed the group: "This side conversation is raising an extremely important point. Either we can use these data to stereotype our children, or we can use them to identify areas where we need to do things differently at the school. We have the choice—either we believe that children have the capacity to learn, or we build artificial barriers for them."

Carolyn said, "I must say, this is an astonishing approach. Ten years ago I was on one of these committees when our oldest child was at this school and the approach then was that given our demographics the children were doing pretty well."

"Yes," Karl responded, "we in education have begun to see that the choice is ours. We can blame the child's neighborhood, parents, culture, et cetera for underachievement, or we can accept no excuses and find out how to teach the children."

✐

Reflection

How are conversations about learners framed where you work? Do you and your colleagues talk in terms of enabling learners? Does the conversation ever shift to external reasons why they don't learn (e.g., culture, socioeconomic status, or level of education)? Think back to a time when you were engaged in conversation with colleagues that focused on why learners were not performing well. Was the focus on the time that the learners were not in the classroom (e.g., sociocultural influences), or was the focus on the time spent with the instructors? Do you tend to gravitate to those things over which you have minimal control or influence or to those that are in your sphere of influence? In other words, are you taking control of the situation, or are you giving up your power?

〜

Activity

In the space provided here, write a list showing what you have heard people say to explain why learners are not performing well. Next, write a corresponding list indicating what happens when you take control and assume responsibility for learner performance.

Why don't learners perform well?

What happens when I assume responsibility for learner performance?

_____

_____

_____

_____

_____

_____

_____

What is your emotional response to these two lists?

_____

_____

_____

_____

_____

_____

_____

_____

Valuing Diversity Is a Sign of Respect

Sign of understanding God's world & creative being

To value diversity is to respect the learners and to encourage them to show respect to one another. As a culturally proficient instructor, you treat learners in ways that the learners perceive as respectful. This may mean using a different criterion for respect than you would for yourself, and explaining the difference to the learners.

Leadership Maple View, a broad-based community project, was designed to identify community-based needs to which the leadership team would respond. By having its members serve one-year terms, Leadership Maple View facilitates networking opportunities for its members. Suzie Cheng, the human relations specialist at Tri-Counties Community College, had been hearing some grumbling about insensitivity at the high school. She conferred with fellow members of Leadership Maple View, who referred her to Sam Brewer and Dr. Barbara Campbell as people who were sensitive to the issues Suzie wanted to address.

Suzie, Sam, and Barbara are meeting in Barbara's office. Both Barbara and Sam know that Suzie wants to talk with them about reported insensitivity from a few teachers. Apparently, the teachers are having difficulty pronouncing new students' names and would either ask them "What do they call you for short?" or "What do they call you at home?" or "What is your American name?" The three agreed that the issue needed to be addressed—now.

Barbara began, "Ms. Cheng, I want to thank you so much for bringing this issue to our attention."

Sam added, "Ms. Cheng, I want you to know how shocked I was to hear your concerns. While I have never personally heard of this happening, I can imagine it happening, and I can also imagine that the teachers are oblivious to how their comments are received."

"Let me say how pleased I am by your responsiveness," Suzie said. "However, let me begin by saying that I am perfectly comfortable being addressed by my first name and I truly appreciate your consideration in addressing me as you have. Yes, this is an issue that, while not intentional, leaves children feeling devalued. What makes it even more complicated is that some children and their parents adopt American names to make it easier for others."

"Yes," Barbara said, "but it seems to me that if we as teachers and administrators take the time to learn how to pronounce someone's name that we are honoring that person and her or his heritage."

"Agreed," Sam said enthusiastically. "I think that it demonstrates our willingness and ability to learn."

"I appreciate your viewpoints," said Suzie. "Also, as teachers and administrators come to know the students, they may well be invited to use other, more familiar names."

"That is a key point. One should be invited to do so." Barbara turned to Sam, "How do you think our colleagues at the high school would react to our raising this issue? What is the best way of doing it?"

"Well, there will be resistance by some few. A presenter last year said that we are still acting as if we are teaching the students who were here a generation ago. This sounds like confirmation of that observation. If it is OK with the two of you, I am going to raise this with our staff development committee. I know we can approach this issue in ways that work for school personnel, as well as for members of our community."

⤙

Reflection

Think back to your most recent experience as a learner. It may have been a professional development session, a college class, or some other setting. How did you experience the way the instructor treated the learners? Did you see instances of disregard? Instances of respect? How do you imagine that learning was affected by this treatment? Can you recall an event in your schooling in which you were treated with disrespect by an instructor? Can you remember the experience? Can you remember your feelings? Are you surprised by how vividly you remember the event and your feelings?

Now, think of an instructor who was quite the opposite. Have you observed an instructor who demonstrated regard for learners, independent of their gender, race, ethnicity, or social class? Describe the learning environment in this scenario.

_____

_____

_____

_____

_____

_____

_____

_____

Take a few moments to look at a current group of learners with whom you are working. Note the areas where you are showing regard for learners and areas in which you would like to improve.

_____

_____

_____

_____

_____

_____

_____

_____

Valuing Diversity Embodies High Expectations

Alicia Alvarez and Rose Diaz-Harris serve on the site council for Maple View Middle School. They are discussing the previous day's site-council meeting, which Rose couldn't attend because she chose to attend an open house at her daughter Susan's school. The teachers at the meeting decided that they wanted to start making home visits to establish rapport with a wider group of parents.

Alicia had mixed feelings about the meeting. On the one hand, she was truly pleased by the teachers' decision. However, she was dismayed by the comments that were made after the announcement. She had heard them say, "Should we dress down? Are the parents going to be embarrassed by having us in their homes? Do we have to eat the food if they offer it?" Alicia felt stunned and embarrassed to hear these comments.

Alicia began, "Really, Rose, I am not interested in complaining about the teachers, but the comments surprised and hurt me. These are my neighbors and our children they were describing."

"Oh, I can see why you are disturbed!" said Rose. "Did any of the people appear to be angry about going? Did you detect any underlying negative feelings?"

"No, that is what is so perplexing. They seemed to be genuinely interested in making the home visits. Now I am afraid they will just make things worse."

"I wish I could have been there," Rose said. "The last thing we want to do is to create a schism between any parents and educators at this school. What I have to do is to get on the agenda for both the site council and the next staff meeting to discuss how we enter people's homes, as their guests. As instructors, our role in this activity is to build bridges. We have to act with that intention, and we have to pay attention to everything we say and do. These kinds of insensitive comments can create insurmountable divisions."

Reflection

Think of a time in your life, professional or personal, when a person made a comment that surprised you and hurt your feelings. Briefly describe the situation and your feelings at the time.

_____

_____

_____

_____

_____

_____

_____

⟿

As an instructor, you learn to continuously monitor your teaching. You gain insight into which parts of the curriculum work and which do not. You learn what works for some learners but not for others. Likewise, when you monitor the language you use, try to detect negative judgments that hide just below the surface. These judgments may reflect your unwitting engagement in cultural incapacity. What makes these judgments powerful is that you may not be aware of what you are doing. This is why cultural proficiency requires both intention and attention.

Valuing Diversity Is Collaborative

To value diversity is to collaborate. Through collaboration, you show that you value the input and concerns of all the stakeholders in your instructional setting. You recognize the value in considering more than one option, and you establish a precedent for supporting more than one approach to reaching a goal. As a culturally proficient instructor, you continuously monitor your learners' progress as a guide to your teaching, and you organize instruction to help the learners become a community of learners.

One experience that most schools and human service agencies have at regular intervals is accreditation by professional and governmental agencies. When done well, these visits can provide educators with data with which to make effective decisions about their organization. These decisions may involve better serving a constituent group, implementing technology to facilitate services, or making long-range plans for staffing needs.

At Pine Hills High School, one of the accreditation guidelines is to disaggregate the data by gender, ethnicity, and social class (based on free and reduced-cost lunch counts). Because of his knowledge of and skill with technology, Sam Brewer has been collecting, arraying, and analyzing data for the high school's upcoming regional accreditation visit. The Faculty-Student-Community (FSC) Committee suggested doing the same for extracurricular activities. When first arrayed, the data showed that students' participation correlated quite highly with their respective numbers in the student body. However, when the disaggregated data was by gender and ethnicity, the result was very interesting.

Addressing the FSC Committee, Sam said, "Let me draw your attention to Chart 1. In this chart, you will note that the participation rates for male and female students are comparable to their populations in school. Then, when you look at the next row, you will note that the participation rate of students when arrayed by ethnicity also shows a participation rate across groups comparable to their representation in the school."

Carolyn, a parent, exclaimed, "Wow! This is great. Both the school and the accrediting agency should love this."

"Yes, both should," said Sam.

David, another parent asked, "But what about our request at the last session to break it down by activities. How did that turn out?"

"Good question," Sam said. "Please turn to Chart 2 on the next page. In this chart, you will see that some activities are definitely 'male' and some are definitely 'female.' Now part of that may be easily explained. However, when you look further, by ethnicity, you will find that some activities involve a high percentage of European American, African American, Latino and Latina, or Asian Pacific students. Note also that a few extracurricular activities are well integrated. Chart 3 extends the analysis to show that students from lower-income families participate very little in school activities."

Paulo, one of the students, feigned a laugh: "You didn't need to do a study to find this out. Any student on campus could have told you this."

"The student's right!" said Sam. "But if we had not had this opportunity to sit down and take this data-driven look at our school, we may have continued to ignore what is so apparent to our students. If there is a value to the FSC Committee, it is this kind of collaboration."

Then Carolyn said, "Like we did with the norm-referenced data, our best strategy is to make observations and ask questions about the data so we can seek ways to improve participation. Is that right?"

David and Sam both responded, "That is what I want."

"And let me continue," said Sam. "This is not about blaming anyone for what we have here. It is about finding ways for all students to be successful at this high school."

Reflection

Remember a time when you organized your class to do group work and the learners were able to solve a complex problem or do a complicated task. What happened? Do you remember the energy level going up? What were some of the moments of frustration? What else did you observe about the interactions?

_____

_____

_____

_____

_____

_____

The Valuing of Diversity Is Tested in Stressful Times

In times of war and great stress, people place less value on diversity. Moreover, as stress increases to the point of hysteria, people begin to fear the differences among them. Remember the economic hysteria in the early 1990s when U.S. citizens realized that Japanese corporations were buying a lot of prime U.S. real estate? Remember the community hysteria that erupted following the spate of school campus shootings, probably best exemplified by the shooting at Columbine High School in Denver, Colorado?

Stressors and crises can also lead to hysteria in the classroom. At times of crisis, culturally proficient instructors recognize the tendency to devalue diversity. In anticipation of such tendencies, culturally proficient instructors help learners to know one another in personal ways that transcend, yet value, cultural differences. In this way, they can reengender a valuing of diversity.

Leadership Maple View was designed to identify community-based needs to which the leadership team would respond. During its first two years, Leadership Maple View improved a city park, constructed pedestrian walkways, and created billboards displaying the city's leadership theme, "Growing Our Own Leaders." Maple View, like many other cities surrounding New Metropolis, had historically had a small nucleus of well-intentioned people running the government. Much of the early success of Leadership Maple View was due to the extensive and ongoing training the participating leaders received. Their training has included training in communication and problem-solving skills in diverse settings.

The Community Survey Subcommittee of Leadership Maple View includes Alberto Alvarez, the assistant manager of MedSupplies.com; Carlos Montanaro, the owner of Maple View Rock and Cement Company; and Don Carlson, manager of the Target Store. This is their first meeting after having received the most recent community survey. The discussion has come to revolve around some previously unrecognized concerns about the proximity of Maple View Elementary School to the Medical Supply Center and MedSupplies.com. Though these organizations are an important source of services and employment to Maple View and other communities in the area, some of the parents had expressed concern about school-age children being exposed to toxic waste in the trash bins. Alberto, Carlos, and Don are discussing the survey results and are preparing a suggested course of action to be presented to the entire committee of Leadership Maple View at its next meeting.

"I must say I am pleased and somewhat surprised that we are taking on this issue," Alberto said.

"Help me understand your surprise," said Carlos. "Isn't that what Leadership Maple View is about?"

"Oh no, I am not trying to be critical," Alberto continued. "But our earlier projects did not have a direct impact on the Maple View community, and Alicia and I are just surprised, and let me hasten to add pleased, by this undertaking."

"Yeah, Carlos," said Don. "I must agree with Alberto. Many of my employees come from the Maple View community, and I have been hearing about this concern for several years."

"I don't want to sound defensive, but has anything happened to any of the children at the school?" Carlos asked.

"No, and no one was shot at Pine Hills High School after the tragedy at Columbine High School, but the community leaders became very vigilant after that." Alberto continued, "Again, please understand me, I am very pleased by the vigilance at the high school and at this effort on behalf of Maple View Elementary. All I am trying to say is that this is new attention for us, though there is some wariness in the community as to whether any good will come from our efforts. Alicia and I will do all we can to make this initiative successful."

"I am stunned," said Carlos. "Not by what you are saying, Alberto, but by the reactions from your community. What I am sitting here wondering is, if we did not have this committee, would these critical issues ever have been addressed? I guess what I am reacting to is my own lack of awareness. Thank you for your forthrightness."

Reflection

How did Alberto experience this conversation about his community to be different from his usual experiences with "the powers that be"? What was Don's experience, through the eyes and ears of his employees? How do you think Carlos was feeling during this conversation?

_____

_____

_____

_____

_____

_____

_____

_____

What insights do you have about how the Maple View Elementary School community has historically been treated within the larger Maple View community? What does the term *invisibility* mean to you?

_____

_____

_____

_____

_____

_____

_____

_____

How do you describe Carlos's receptivity to these historical allusions? How do you contrast Alberto's feelings now with his earlier experiences in the community?

_____

_____

_____

_____

_____

_____

✐

Reflection

Think of a time when you or someone you know well had a negative experience that colleagues in your organization did not see. Then think of a time when someone's experience was recognized and valued. Write a few words that describes each situation, and draw the distinctions between them. Note instances of when people took care to value the differences among others.

_____

_____

_____

_____

_____

✐

To Value Diversity Is to Value Difference

Noticing, appreciating, and respecting differences is fundamental to val-uing diversity. In your own classroom, you can see differences and simi-larities expressed and accepted as equally important aspects of every-one's learning.

D r. Barbara Campbell has been overseeing the implementa-tion of the diversity workshops for employees of the Maple View School District. She worked with the Diversity Staff Devel-opment Committee to develop criteria for the selection of consul-tants. Principally, they wanted consultants who could help the employees be more responsive to the various cultures represented in the classrooms and community. Secondarily, they wanted con-sultants to initiate activities that would influence the develop-ment of more inclusive curricula.

At one of the diversity workshops sponsored by the district, the consultant had posted around the training room posters with these headings: "African American Men," "African American Women," "Latinos," "Latinas," "White Men," "White Women," "Gay Men," and "Lesbians," among others. Participants were invited to take packets of sticky notes and to mill around the room, writing and affixing to the posters various stereotypes they had heard about the respective groups.

Following the workshop, Howard Smith, an African Ameri-can high school teacher, was so upset about the activity that he made an appointment to speak with Barbara Campbell. Howard was deeply troubled that differences and similarities can be expressed and accepted as two equally important parts of all peo-ple's learning. During their meeting, Howard objected strenu-ously to comparing stereotypes of African Americans with those of Gay men and Lesbians.

"Dr. Campbell," Howard began, "I do not want to partici-pate in diversity activities that seek to compare the experiences of all groups as being comparable."

Barbara said, "I saw the consultant trying to draw comparisons to stereotypes and the negative effects of stereotypes. I didn't see her trying to make experiences comparable."

"Well, I did, and I am not going to stand for it!" Howard was adamant.

"Howard, do you mean to tell me that as a high school teacher, you are going to engage in a type of 'oppression Olympics'? Though we have had different histories, isn't the object of this activity to keep us from doing to others what has been done to us? In my mind, that does not keep us from knowing and studying our various historical and current experiences. I would think that a good teacher like you would want your students to know the unique experiences of other groups, as well as how those experiences compare across history."

"You have a point," said Howard. "I didn't hear it that way yesterday. It is too bad that consultant didn't express it as clearly as you just did."

"The example I just gave you is the same one she gave you yesterday. You could not hear it from her, but you can now from me. Why do you think you can hear it now?"

"To be honest?"

"Of course."

"I thought she was running her own agenda!"

"Howard, over the many years that you have been a teacher, how often have you heard that same allegation made about us?"

"Aaarrrggghhh. I hear you! I guess I have to avoid getting into the trap of thinking that similarities and differences are opposites. They can, and do, exist in our lives."

Reflection

Remember a time when someone judged the way you did a task and did not inquire about why you did it that way. Think of a time when you experienced something as different and immediately judged it harshly instead of acknowledging it as a manifestation of diversity. Think of insights you have made about learners in your classrooms when you discovered something about them that you initially judged negatively, only to find that it illustrated how they approached learning differently than you had expected. In the space provided, record your reactions and how you would like to have seen the situation handled differently.

_____

_____

⟿

To value diversity is to recognize that each culture finds some values more important than others. As a culturally proficient instructor, you know that some learners value getting the right answer, whereas others want to know how the answer was derived. You recognize that some learners prefer to work alone, whereas others prefer to work in pairs or in groups.

Pine Hills Elementary School had been experiencing a small in-migration of Latino students from Central American countries. Joaquin Jarrin, a sixth-grade teacher there, had a parent conference that left him confused. He had asked for the conference with the parent of his student Josefina, to try to determine why she was doing so poorly on a literature and history project. All year long, she had been one of his best students, and her work on this project was clearly below her potential. The conference left him befuddled, so he asked Eduardo Gonzales, one of the third-grade teachers at Maple View Elementary School, to help him sort out what had happened.

"Ed, I am totally confused. Josefina has done exceptionally well all year, until this project. In talking with her parent, all I could discern was that Josefina would not be writing anything that would criticize others."

"What was the project, Joaquin?"

"It is one I have done for several years. I provide the students with source material that offers different perspectives on a historical event. Using the literature of the day, and a rubric, they are to critique the various perspectives. What I want them to learn is to read and analyze critically."

"Ah, that may be the issue. In some cultures, it is considered presumptuous, even rude, to criticize material provided by the school."

"That's interesting, Ed. I didn't know that. So, I have to teach that critiquing and criticizing are not necessarily the same. In fact, I have to help Josefina and her parent to see that this is an important skill, for use both in education and in being an informed citizen."

"I think you are onto something now."

⟜

Reflection

Think of a time in your personal life when you discovered that someone who was very important to you did not value something in the same way you did. Was it about being on time to an event? Was it about including details in a report or project? If the conflict was with your spouse or partner, was it about deciding on a vacation?

Now, look at your current classroom. Do you see that you and some of your learners have different views on a specific value? Do you differ about starting precisely on time? Do you differ about the amount of detail you provide when assigning tasks? Is it about how you present lessons? Is it about different passions or interests regarding the topic?

In the space provided, briefly describe one particular incident. Next, write why it is important to you. Then project how the learners in your classroom would view the same situation. Notice the similarities and differences. To what extent do the differences and similarities directly influence the subject being taught as opposed to the styles used in teaching and learning? What matters most?

_____

_____

_____

_____

_____

_____

⟞

Sam Brewer stopped by Dr. Barbara Campbell's office late one afternoon, hoping to find her to talk with her about her role with the Diversity Staff Development Committee. Barbara was pleased to see Sam in the office and was encouraged by his comments on how well the training was going. His real motive for being there, however, was to question his own role and behaviors on the committee. Sam was wondering whether he had what it takes to deal with the varied and sometimes contentious issues around diversity.

"Dr. Campbell, you always seem to know exactly what to say in the training or with parents or teachers or community members to keep them focused on the positive side of diversity. I'm not sure I'll ever be able to do that. What else can I do to learn more about valuing diversity?"

"Sam, you are being too hard on yourself. Do you think it takes a person of color to value diversity?"

"No, not exactly, but I can't speak with the same experience and credibility that you have."

"And you are not expected to. You bring your own experiences. And your credibility is based on the high value you place on diversity, the important work that you do in opening the minds and hearts of the people you work with, affirming that differences are not deficits. That is what gives you credibility, Sam. Your work demonstrates your values."

Going Deeper

What have you learned from Sam? What have you learned from the vignettes in this chapter? After reflecting on what you learned from this chapter, develop an activity for your colleagues to help enhance their understanding of what "valuing diversity" really means.

_____

_____

_____

_____

_____

_____

_____

_____

_____

_____

_____

_____

_____

8

Managing the Dynamics of Difference

Reframing the Differences

We will not all agree, but perhaps we can start by examining what keeps us from hearing viewpoints that differ from our own.

onflict is a basic, natural aspect of life. For a moment, think of conflict as tension. To walk, you must coordinate the tensing and relaxing muscles in your body—including the beating of your heart muscles. Tension and conflict are vital to life, as well as to almost every other process in our universe.

Imagine a world in which everyone was exactly like you and liked everything that you liked. After a week or two, most of us would long for company that would challenge, test, entertain, or complement us. Conflict makes the world work. Without tension and the conflict that accompanies it, we would lose the benefits of creative brainstorming, group problem solving, and collective decision making. So why, then, do so many of us think that conflict is bad? Why do we often view conflict as a negative? Perhaps because so few of us have the necessary skills to manage conflict well.

⊷

Getting Centered

Think of a classroom conflict in which you are currently embroiled or that you resolved recently. How well do you think you are handling it—or handled it? What resources do/did you have for managing it? What do you think is/was the source of the conflict?

_____

_____

_____

_____

_____

_____

⊷

Mismanaging Conflict

It is the mismanagement of conflict, not the conflict itself, that causes most problems. In dominant American society, we are socialized to perceive conflict as something to avoid. Most of us have problems because we haven't learned to manage the conflict that precipitated the problem. Instead, we learn to ignore the conflict and maintain superficial niceties, to be polite instead of honest, to sweep conflict under the rug and dance around the huge heap of elephant dung in the middle of the room. When those tactics no longer work, we become aggressors or adversaries, and we seek someone or something to blame for our dilemmas. Once you understand that conflict is normal and natural, you will not like it any more than you do now, but you will then be ready to seek ways to understand it and to manage it more effectively.

In a classroom, conflict abounds. When you are relating to people in a classroom setting, you start out with a power conflict. The instructor usually has more power than the learners do. As the instructor, you control what is taught, how it is taught, and what the learners must do to receive your teaching. You choose among presentation techniques (e.g., lecture, reading, small groups, use of media, experiential activities). You determine where people sit, when they can take breaks, and how their learning will be assessed. As the instructor, you may not feel as powerful as you are perceived to be, and that is another source of conflict.

You seek to have a sense of control over your classroom environment. Often, however, your supervisor seeks some control over your classroom and your instruction. Whether you work in an elementary school or are the lead trainer in a bank, someone is probably trying to have control over or input into what you teach, the materials you teach with, and in many cases how you teach.

Often, people who are seeking to stay in control do not have the skills to manage the conflicts that arise between them and the people who also seek to control their environments. When people have greater institutional power, they often make rules to ensure that they get their way or that the symptoms of the resulting conflict do not affect them. This is very common in the classroom. When instructors do not have the skill to manage conflict effectively, they often make rules instead.

S tuart Montgomery, a teacher at Pine View Middle School, is angry because two students took advantage of their hall pass privileges. "OK, we've been having this problem for too long, so from now on, no one will be allowed to use the hall pass during class. So people, take care of your business before class or after class. Once you walk through that door, you are mine until the bell rings. The only excuse for missing class is death, and if you die during class, you will still wait until the class is over to leave."

You probably recognize this high school example as a bit extreme, but you may also laugh because it is all too familiar. As instructors, we make rules about where people sit, forcing them to move to the front and center of the room—for our comfort. We pass out papers one sheet at a time so that our learners will not read ahead. We insist that they take notes—or not take notes. We insist that their posture signals rapt attention—so that we are assured that our messages are getting across. We do this despite our years of study about the differences in how people think and listen and process information. Moreover, we do this in classrooms

that are relatively homogeneous. What happens when you choose to acknowledge the differences in the classroom? What happens when you
invite a diversity of learners into the training room?

Once you have embraced a value for diversity, conflict management
poses even more challenges (Banks, 1999; McAllister & Jordan Irvine,
2000; Riehl, 2000). By acknowledging diversity, you now recognize more
people, with more differences, and you consequently have more issues
over which to disagree. When you and I sit down to the table for a conversation (whoever you and I may be), we both have to remember that
not only do we bring ourselves to the table, but we bring our personal
histories as well. Our personal histories lead to conscious or unconscious
awareness. For example, I may have issues with people who are X, and
you may feel uncomfortable around people who do Y.

Each of us brings our biases and prejudices that provide the lenses
through which we see and interpret everything. Also present at the table
are the ghosts of our past experiences dealing with this particular issue
and of our past experiences dealing with people like the person whom
we face. We also bring to the table the ghosts of our parents, our families,
and our friends who influence, however subtly, the way we give, receive,
and interpret information. Knowing and acknowledging these realities
about ourselves enables us to become culturally proficient.

Because you value diversity, you assess the variety of differences
present in your classroom, assess the potential for conflict, and work to
acquire skills to manage it. You may be familiar with the term *conflict resolution*. This term implies that conflict can be ended. Sometimes that is
true. Most of the time, however, conflict can only be managed. That is,
you cannot make the issue causing the conflict to go away, but you can
help people to develop healthy responses to it. For these reasons, we prefer the term *conflict management.*

⟞

Reflection

Think about the conflict you described in the "Getting Centered"
activity for this chapter. Was it your conflict with a learner or group of
learners? Was it between groups of learners? Do you believe that, perhaps, the issue was more serious than it appeared at first? Describe the
behaviors and feelings that you observed. Don't analyze them; just
describe them.

_____

_____

_____

_____

_____

_____

_____

⟵

As you read the next section, keep this situation in mind. You will be invited to take a closer look at it later in this chapter.

Sources of Conflict

To manage conflict effectively, first determine the nature of the conflict. There are six basic categories over which people have conflicts: facts, values, perceptions, methods, personalities, and cultures (Schein, 1989). *Facts* are indisputable truths. If you are in conflict over what you think are facts, get the real facts. Collect the facts, correct what you thought were facts, and sort them from values and perceptions.

Values are strongly held beliefs that do not require facts to support them; our values are filters through which we observe what goes on in our environment. If values are the source of the conflict, it is important to clarify them and understand that it is almost impossible to change another person's values. Seek to understand different values, but don't waste time attempting to change them. People do not change their values because someone has presented them with a persuasive argument. We change our values because of significant emotional events, such as birth, death, marriage, divorce, or life crises. Our values also change over time when we interact with someone or something that conflicts with our values and causes us to rethink a previously nonnegotiable belief.

Perceptions are our interpretations of the facts that our senses show us. Often, people mistake their perceptions for facts. If differences in perception are the cause of the conflict, check your perceptions and those of others, and share them. Invite the other parties to sit where you are so that they can see the object of conflict from your perspective. At the same time, move to where the other parties are so that you can view the object from their perspective. Clarify each observer's perceptions so that you can understand why each of you has taken your respective positions.

Ury (1991) calls this perspective taking "going to the balcony." In the theater, if you have a seventh-row center seat, you are in the best position to appreciate the sets and the makeup and the lighting. You can willfully suspend your disbelief because your perspective is perfect to appreciate the magic of the theater. If, however, you are in the balcony, your perspective changes dramatically. You may suspend your disbelief, but you may also be distracted by what else you can see. From the balcony, you have a glimpse around the sets, and you can see what is behind them. You may see the many workers who help to make the magic. You can see the lights and the pulleys that move the sets; you can see the orchestra in the pit. Because of your perspective, your understanding and appreciation of what is happening on the stage are very different than they were in your seventh-row center seat. When you go to the balcony in the midst of a conflict, you are stepping off the center stage of the drama so that you can see a bit more. Often, with greater understanding comes greater appreciation. It is then much easier to separate perceptions from facts.

Suppose that your supervisor assigned 45 students to your classroom. You may perceive that your supervisor did so to punish you with extra students. Your philosophy of teaching, which is informed by your values, tells you that this overcrowding is wrong: Learners cannot thrive in an environment in which you are forced to lecture because you believe there is no space or time to teach in any other way. If you are concerned about the great number of people in your classroom, ask your supervisor, "Please help me to understand why I now have 45 people in my class, when we agreed that 20 was the optimal number?" You may learn that you are not, in fact, being punished, but that this was a way to resolve some other problem that your supervisor had. You, on the other hand, reply that had your supervisor inquired, you could have provided a number of alternative solutions. You and he are now in a conflict of methodology.

Conflict in *methods* often results in an argument over whose methods will be used. Here, you need to negotiate. Is the objective to do things according to a particular process or to get a specific product? Get agreement on what is important: the process or the product. If it is the product, be sure you have established criteria for evaluating the end product, and let the people involved in the process decide which method they will use for getting that product. Again, how the conflict is managed may be influenced by who has the most institutional power or how each person in the situation perceives the power of the other. It gets complicated, but it is a negotiation that takes place daily for most people.

If you find that you are in conflict because of *different personality styles*, it is important to understand the motivating factors behind the personality. Is the person gentle or forceful, oriented toward people or toward products? Have you noticed whether your language tends to be concrete or abstract? Do you process ideas randomly or sequentially? There are many assessment tools that can help you to determine what your social style is. Your goal here is to adjust your approach to complement the other person's style of interacting so that you will be better able to focus on the issues that concern you both.

Differences in *culture* cover a wide range of values and behaviors, and we have no consistent matrices for culture. Conflicts in values, perceptions, or methods may emerge because of differences in age, gender, geography, social class, or ability. Just as you will not change anyone's values, you will not change anyone's culture. To get through the conflicts arising from these differences, you must first notice that the differences among people do make a difference. Then, in collaboration with the other person, seek to understand what differences are causing conflict and then decide what would be best for the current situation. Strive to increase your own and the other person's understanding and, consequently, willingness to work toward mutually acceptable goals. This approach works reasonably well when the conflict is between two people with a sophisticated collection of conflict management tools.

With a larger and presumably more diverse group, you will need a wider range of conflict management skills. If you have good conflict management skills now, congratulations. We invite you to develop a still higher level of skills so that you can manage the subtle nuances of cultural differences. The principle of intentionality, proceeding with the conscious intention of doing something differently, applies here. The more intention and attention you give to the process, the more positive will be the outcomes you achieve. If your intention is to notice the different ways that people respond to your questions, you will learn, over time, to recognize or inquire when you suspect that the men and women give gender-specific responses to certain types of questions. You may notice that the questions the middle-aged professional is asking are not an indictment of your poor teaching skills but, rather, a plea to be noticed and recognized for what he or she knows.

The Leadership Maple View committee has been meeting to determine the scope of its new project. Committee members have expressed their own views and ideas about the current leadership theme, "Growing Our Own Leaders." Dr. Franklin Jackson, president of Tri-Counties Community College, served as moderator for the opening sessions and the keynote speaker for the kickoff event. However, Dr. Jackson has not attended any of the work sessions of the committee. In his absence, Dr. Barbara Campbell has been asked to facilitate the committee meetings and the work of the group.

Dr. Campbell begins the fourth meeting of the group: "The purpose of tonight's meeting is to reach consensus about the leadership project for this year. We have heard several suggestions in our previous meetings, all of which are consistent with the charge given us by Dr. Jackson at our first meeting. Let's continue to brainstorm other ideas; then we can clarify these ideas and narrow the list to determine our top priorities and, finally, choose the project on which we will focus our energy and resources for the year."

"Dr. Campbell," said Carlos Montanaro, "I like how you have outlined our work here tonight. Many of us have busy work schedules, and having this clear purpose will help us get right down to our new project."

"Yeah, me too," said Stu Montgomery. "Those of us who are teachers hardly have time to do any of the extra community stuff as it is. So, let's talk about who wants to do what. I think we need to do something to help the poor families over on the East Side catch up with their schoolwork. We could probably set up some community sports clubs, too, to help out some of the families over there."

"Excuse me, Mr. Montgomery," Alberto Alvarez interrupted, "but you make it sound like 'over there' is not even part of Maple View. As a matter of fact, the East Side was the only side until a few years ago. People like my father helped build this community, and he would want us to work together on this leadership project. You make it sound like the poor people on the East Side need some special attention."

"Now wait a minute," Stu protested. "That is not what I said at all. Your people are highly respected in this town. You have worked hard for everthing you have. It is just that some people don't really care about what their kids do after school or in the neighborhood. Some parents don't care how their kids do in school. We have to help those kids."

"Mr. Montgomery," said Alicia Alvarez, "I wish more teachers would take the time to learn about what parents really think and care about, before they assume that parents don't care. I know that some parents care greatly for their children and they trust the lives of their children to the teachers and schools of this community. Do you think the parents on the West Side care more about their children than the parents on the East Side of town?"

"Hey, now wait a minute . . . ." Stu protested, "this isn't fair. . . . I'm not a racist . . . ." Dr. Campbell stepped in, "OK, hold on Stu. No one called you a racist. Members of the committee have brought up some interesting questions. Maybe it is time that we dealt with what some folks in this city call the 'East Side secret.' Stu, I heard your defensive comments, and I believe that they come from your sincere desire to serve the children of this city. These are emotional issues that the committee must be willing to deal with. Our community deals with them daily. My hope is that we are willing to present our views and ideas in an open and honest forum. We will not all agree, but perhaps we can start by examining what keeps us from hearing viewpoints that differ from our own. Now, I'll chart some of the issues that I've heard here tonight so that we can continue to keep them in front of us."

Let's review the six conflict management strategies:

1. Get the facts.
2. Clarify values.
3. Check perceptions.
4. Negotiate methods.
5. Adjust to personalities.
6. Seek to understand cultural differences.

Chart 8.1 invites you to look at these conflict management strategies from both the individual and the organizational perspectives.

Reflection

Review the conflict situation you identified in the "Getting Centered" activity for this chapter. Can you describe the source of the conflict in each of your own examples? Look at Chart 8.1, and see whether you used an appropriate strategy for addressing the conflict.

_____

_____

_____

_____

_____

_____

_____

_____

_____

_____

⤙

Strategies for Managing Conflict

The preceding section described the sources of conflict; we now invite you to focus on the various ways that people manage conflict. To manage conflict requires courage, trust, and commitment; it also requires you to apply the principle of intentionality. You cannot wish conflict away, or simply hope that you will manage it. Instead, you must attend closely to the people and the situation, and you must begin with the intention of managing the tension. You must think about what you want and then anticipate how you might act differently to manage the tension in that particular situation.

As an instructor, not only do you have situations in which you are in conflict with someone—your colleague, your supervisor, or one of the learners in your classroom—but you are also called on to mediate conflicts between people in your classroom. Each of us has a preferred style

CHART 8.1 *Management Strategies for Various Sources of Conflict*

Sources of Conflict	Management Strategy	For Individuals		For Organizations	
		Within the Person	Between Persons	Within the Organization	Between Organizations
Facts	Determine what the facts actually are.		x	x	x
Values	Distinguish your core values from your strong opinions. Communicate your values clearly, remembering that people don't easily change their values and that sometimes you may have to engage in activities that conflict with your personal values.	x	x	x	x
Perceptions	Separate your perceptions from the facts. Ask questions to learn how the other person perceives the situation.	x	x	x	x
Methods	Ask yourself, is your way important, or is it just important that you have your way?	x	x	x	x
Personalities	Recall your understanding of social styles to make the appropriate adjustments.		x		
Cultures	Engage in a learning conversation to discern why you want to do something or engage with someone in a particular way. Decide with the other party what would best serve everyone's needs in the particular situation.		x	x	x

for managing conflict. Those of us who handle conflict effectively use a style that is appropriate for the situation. The five most common styles of conflict management are avoidance, accommodation, compromise, competition, and collaboration.

When *avoiding* conflict, people do not immediately pursue their own concerns or those of the other person. They simply do not address the conflict. This avoidance may take the form of diplomatically sidestepping an issue, postponing an issue until a better time, or simply withdrawing from a threatening situation. You are avoiding conflict if you don't deal with the troublesome issue, and you continue to let the conflict simmer in the background. Avoiding often becomes a lose-lose situation because neither of you gets what you want, and both of you may end up losing the relationship. Avoidance is effective when you are not vested in the relationship and you don't care about the issue. If you have a learner who constantly baits you or others in the room, you may avoid the conflict by not recognizing that learner. On the other hand, if two learners are constantly bickering, avoiding a confrontation with them will only lead to further classroom disruptions.

When *accommodating*, people subsume their own concerns to satisfy the concerns of the other person; there is an element of self-sacrifice in this style. Accommodation may take the form of selfless generosity or charity, obeying another person's unpleasant or undesirable order, or yielding to another's point of view. You are accommodating when you go along with the other person because you don't want to make waves. This is a win some-lose some situation. You lose the issue to the other person; the other person loses the benefit of your ideas and perceptions, and you both win a little peace and the perception of harmony. If you are trying to teach a new concept by using a technique that is effective but that the learners don't particularly like, you may win congeniality points by giving in, but you also lose teaching time, and the learners may lose an important learning experience.

When *compromising*, people seek to find some expedient, mutually acceptable solution that partially satisfies both parties. It falls on a middle ground between competing and accommodating. Compromise strategies address an issue more directly than avoidance strategies do. On the other hand, compromise strategies don't explore the issue in as much depth as collaboration strategies do. Compromising might mean splitting the difference, exchanging concessions, or seeking a quick middle-ground position. You give a little to get a little. So does the other person. Compromise is also a win some-lose some situation. Each of you gets something that you want, and each of you loses something that you want. Instructors in K through 12 schools do this all the time, as they bargain with their students for compliance and cooperation. At some point in the careers of instructors who have compromise as their dominant style, they have to make tough choices between covering the breadth of material in their curriculum or taking fewer topics and covering them in depth so that the learners can use the information outside of the classroom.

When *competing*, people pursue their own concerns at the other person's expense, and they use whatever seems appropriate to win their own position. The outcome of this power-oriented management strategy may depend on a person's ability to argue, the person's position, or even threats of harm. Competing might mean standing up for your rights, defending a position that you believe is correct, or simply trying to win. You should compete when the issue is so important that you are willing to risk losing everything in order to win. This is often a lose-lose approach because even if you win, you may lose the relationship because of the tactics you used to win. The best instructors we have observed use cooperative learning strategies far more often than competitive ones. The reduced level of tension and the increased learner-to-learner interaction results in an environment that is conducive to moving toward cultural proficiency.

When *collaborating*, people try to work with one another to find some solution that fully satisfies the concerns of both persons. It means digging into an issue to identify the underlying concerns of the two individuals and to find an alternative that addresses both sets of concerns. Collaboration between two persons may take the form of exploring a disagreement to learn from each other's insights, resolving some condition that would otherwise require them to compete for resources, or confronting and trying to find a creative solution to an interpersonal problem. You should collaborate when the issue and the relationship are equally important to you. Collaboration requires that you invest the time to sort facts and perceptions, to prioritize the issues, to clarify what you really want, and then to figure out a way for you both to get what you want (Thomas & Kilman, 1974).

Because collaboration takes a great deal of time and energy, we do not recommend that you collaborate on every issue. When the relationship is as important as the issue, the investment in collaboration pays off. Collaboration is important as instructors work with other professionals to set long-range goals, determine curriculum, and learn new instructional strategies. Similarly, collaboration is beneficial to the classroom when the instructor uses these skills to engage learners in problem-solving and discovery-learning activities. In these situations, learners will acquire effective communication and problem-solving skills while working with others to solve complex tasks or problems.

⇁

Reflection

What is a situation in your work environment in which collaboration was used to manage a conflict? What have been some situations in your classroom when you have used collaborative teaching strategies? What benefit have you seen for the learners in these situations?

_____

_____

_____

_____

_____

_____

_____

_____

_____

_____

_____

_____

_____

⇁

Activity

Figure 8.1 illustrates five different approaches to managing conflict. Go back to your examples, and see whether your approach was appropriate for the situation, for your intention, and for the attention you gave to the situation.

Figure 8.1. *Approaches to Managing Conflict*

To go higher on the pyramid, you need willingness, intention, assertiveness, cooperation, trust, time to sort issues, time to invest in the relationship, and courage.

⟼

Going Deeper

How do you describe your style of dealing with conflict? How is conflict handled in your classroom? How is it addressed among your colleagues? What skills do you currently possess in this area? What skills would you like to develop?

_____

_____

_____

_____

_____

_____

_____

_____

_____

_____

_____

_____

_____

_____

⟼

9

Adapting to Diversity

Training About Differences

Adapting to diversity is like being in a committed relationship. Both partners have to adjust and change; neither partner remains the same.

It is very easy to decide to change. You say, "Sure," to yourself or who-ever is pestering you, and you stay the same. Making a commitment to change, however, is quite different. When you make a commitment to change, you must work hard to realign your activities and your approach to life to accommodate that change.

Change is easiest when you are in total control of whatever you're changing. You probably rather like it when you decide to rearrange the furniture in your home or when you decide to be with friends instead of family for a holiday celebration. As long as you live alone and reside in a location many hours from your family, you can implement these deci-sions without having to consult with anyone and without any major repercussions. Moreover, besides the physical exertion of moving furni-ture, you can decide to change and then implement the change with very little effort. Too bad that not all change is this easy.

↤

Getting Centered

Have you ever told yourself you wanted to change without really intending to do anything differently? Think of a time you made a decision to be different. Perhaps you decided to exercise more, to go on a diet, or to stop smoking. Did these changes affect anyone other than you? Did you need anyone else's cooperation to implement the change? What steps did you take to ensure that you would change? Did you make the change you set out to make? What do you suppose is the difference between a decision and a commitment?

_____

_____

_____

_____

_____

_____

_____

↤

Making a Personal Commitment to Change

The easiest thing to change is your mind. You can do that lying in bed, half-asleep, watching late-night television. It is much harder to change your behavior and to make the change last over time. It is also much more difficult to change when your change depends on the cooperation of others or when the change requires you to acquire a new set of behaviors. Anyone can stop smoking or go on a diet for the next 15 minutes, but to consistently engage in the new behavior for the next 15 months requires a very different type of effort and commitment.

Again, the principle of intentionality, proceeding with the conscious intention of doing something differently, applies to the commitment to change. To implement a change, you must pay attention to how you are doing things now, then make a conscious decision to do things differently. The more specific you are about how differently you will do things, the greater your likelihood of actually doing it. You must also engage in each situation that calls for the new behavior with the intention of doing so in a different way.

Reflection

Are you engaged in a change today? Have you made a noncommittal decision or a true commitment? To whom?

_____

_____

_____

_____

_____

_____

_____

Your commitment to change is the key to becoming culturally proficient. Cultural proficiency is a process; becoming culturally proficient is not a one-time event like moving your furniture around. It is more like quitting smoking or going on a diet, in that each day you have to decide again whether this is what you want to do. It is a change of lifestyle, in how you view the world around you.

You must become aware of the situations that invite culturally proficient behavior and then pay attention to them so that your behavior will
be different—each time. Becoming culturally proficient requires you to
change on a number of levels. The first level is overcoming your
unawareness of the need to adapt, which we described in Chapter 4, on
barriers to cultural proficiency. Thus, you must first recognize that your
current actions are not having the effect you would like in a particular
environment. Next, you move through the essential elements as you seek
to relate to this environment with cultural proficiency.

Making an Organizational Commitment to Change

By assessing culture—your own culture and that of your organization—
you begin to understand how your instructional behaviors and the organization's practices affect people—both members of the dominant group
and members of nondominant groups. By valuing diversity, you become
more aware of how your prejudices and stereotypes influence the judgments you make and the way you treat the learners you teach. Your
greater awareness, coupled with your conflict management skills, helps
you manage the dynamics of difference.

At this point, your environment may be a little unstable. It is time
now for you to adapt to diversity. By adapting to diversity, you will make
some permanent changes in your values and behaviors and in your organization's policies and practices. These changes will reflect how you and
the diverse people in your environment adapt to one another.

Suzie Cheng is talking to her planning team at Tri-Counties
Community College. They are planning a retreat, and a few
members are complaining about the new site for the retreat. They
cannot go to the mountainside site they have used for years
because it is not wheelchair accessible, and the newest faculty
member, Colleen, needs a wheelchair. Suzie responds, "We have
to make decisions that say everyone is welcome."

Her supervisor asked, "Can't we just appoint two guys to
carry Colleen up and down the stairs?"

"No, our job is not to make an example out of the person we
are accommodating. We must set an example for all the faculty.
Furthermore, we must send a message to the retreat site. They
need to know that we are not coming because they cannot provide

for all of us—and they should! Besides," Suzie continues, "we don't know who else might come. There are people who are not in wheelchairs who may not have come in the past because they have difficulty with the hills and the stairs. These faculty members are not our guests. We cannot treat them as if they will be going away. We've invited them to be a part of our family, so we must adapt to their needs."

Reflection

Think about your school or organization. Can you remember a time in the recent past when you or your organization failed to adapt to the needs of a new member? What is an example of something you or your organization did to adapt to the needs of a new member? How about in your classroom? What examples can you think of when you adapted or failed to adapt to the needs of some learners?

_____

_____

_____

_____

_____

_____

In the vignette, Suzie made a decision to move toward cultural proficiency as an individual and as a member of an organization. However, even her supervisor, who had hired her to help the organization address its diversity issues, had trouble with her decisions. Once you and your organization decide to become more culturally proficient, you must also decide how serious you are about actually becoming culturally proficient because to take action requires more than a change of mind and more than a decision.

Change requires a commitment from the organization, as well as from the individuals who work there. In a committed, monogamous relationship, the partners make a covenant with each other. Their vows are sacred, and implied in the promises they make to each other is the agreement that they will change to accommodate each other's presence in their lives. Clearly, a marriage commitment requires a great deal of effort if the relationship is to work.

Similarly, the commitment to achieving cultural proficiency in your organization requires continual hard work. You must relentlessly look deeply at your own biases, values, and behaviors. You must constantly watch for both overt and benign discrimination in organizational policies and must continually assess the cultural competency of your organization's practices.

At one of the monthly meetings of Leadership Maple View, current members are listening to Nikos Papadopoulos, their diversity consultant, talk to them about cultural proficiency. Nikos is encouraging them to move beyond planning cultural events and special activities around ethnic-specific holidays. The group is flummoxed. For years, the chamber of commerce has sponsored an ethnic food fair in the downtown area. This year, Leadership Maple View plans to cosponsor the event. They already have plans to bring in mariachi bands, African drummers, a bagpipe orchestra, and the New Metropolis Tongan Dancers. They are so proud of all their plans to celebrate the diversity of Maple View.

"What are we supposed to do now," Leonard Williams groaned, "cancel our plans?"

"No," replied Nikos. "Don't cancel your plans. Just realize that once you have knowledge, nothing is going to look the same to you. As you move toward cultural proficiency, you will continue to assess and rethink activities that you have taken for granted in the past. What I was trying to do is invite you to focus more on yourselves. Who are you as a cultural entity? How does 'who you are' affect the people around you? What are the various cultures represented in your classrooms and training rooms? How do they interplay and interact with one another?"

"Wait a minute," Julie exclaimed. "What does culture have to do with teaching math or English literature or banking procedures?"

"And how can we ask nurses to learn about all the cultures that pass through this hospital?" Alicia piped in. "And you know that we can never make doctors do anything. They already think they know everything. We want to do better, but with this cultural proficiency, you are asking us to change the way we do everything!"

Reflection

What questions would you ask the consultant? If you were the consultant, how would you respond? In your school or organization, what is done now to overtly address the issues arising from diversity? In your view, what else needs to be done as a first step?

_____

_____

_____

_____

_____

_____

_____

When an organization makes a commitment to cultural proficiency, everybody must change. This requirement explains why most organizations do not move far beyond special events that celebrate ethnic diversity. As you move toward cultural proficiency, go deeper as organizations and as individuals. Explore and acknowledge the subtler, yet more profound aspects of culture. Look beyond physical type and language to see the difference that differences make on an everyday basis. As with any other committed relationship, you and the other participants in your organization engage in a constant give and take, as each of you adjusts to the other. As a culturally proficient instructor, you must facilitate major and minor adjustments in the culture of your school or organization and in your classroom as well.

Making an Instructional Commitment to Change

Adaptations to diversity are sometimes easier to see at the level of organizational policy and practices, and they may be more difficult to observe in your own classroom behavior. Take a moment now to examine the values that inform how you do the following:

- Select materials for instruction
- Decide on your techniques for presenting materials
- Watch for how learners subtly respond to your choices
- Facilitate healthy conversations among the learners
- Mediate conflicts among learners
- Take advantage of teachable moments, such as these . . .

"The blond bimbo in the back of the room just said . . ."

"I don't have any problem with the homosexuals that I work with, I just don't want them near me."

For the first 2 days of a 10-day training class, one of the learners sat in the back of the room, and whenever she spoke, she used a sexy, throaty, Marilyn Monroe voice. After a few such whispery comments, the instructor started being really annoyed with the woman. "Please," the instructor implored, "speak so people can hear you." "Speak up please," the instructor reminded her each time. At the beginning of the third day, the woman approached the instructor and said, "You keep insisting that I speak up for everyone to hear. I just wanted you to know that not all handicaps are visible. I have damaged vocal chords and cannot speak above my stage whisper."

⟼

Reflection

What do you see as the adaptation issues in these teachable moments? How would you respond to each example?

_____

_____

_____

_____

_____

_____

_____

⟼

In Chapter 8, on managing the dynamics of difference, we discussed the dynamics of power in the classroom. As an instructor, you have the power that comes from your role, and most of the learners accede to that power. As we're sure you know, the learners have a lot of power as well. They have the power of noncooperation, the power to disrupt, the power of noncompliance, the power to withdraw or not participate, and the power to not show up.

In elementary classrooms, learners often play an overt game of bullying and one-upmanship with their fellow classmates. In a classroom of adults, the games are still played, but the tactics are subtler and the consequences more profound. Sometimes, as instructors, we encounter learners who bring out the worst in us. We respond by bullying, picking on them, and refusing to acknowledge them when they seek to contribute in the classroom. As a culturally proficient instructor, you will recognize when you are overusing your power or using it inappropriately, and you will change what you do to adapt to the diversity in your classroom.

⟶

Reflection

These questions may be difficult for you. In your classroom, who is the oppressor, and who are the oppressed? If you say no one, spend a few days observing yourself and your learners. Who has the power, and how is it used? Who is scapegoated, teased, ignored, interrupted, ridiculed, punished, or penalized? Do you notice any patterns? How does the scapegoats' behavior differ from that of the other learners in the classroom? Are the scapegoats really doing anything wrong? Who does the scapegoating, teasing, ignoring, interrupting, ridiculing, punishing, and penalizing? What must change?

_____

_____

_____

_____

_____

_____

⟶

From a Christmas Party to a Winter Celebration

A hallmark of the culturally proficient organization is its ability to adapt to change. One public way that organizations adapt to diversity is to change the way holidays are recognized and celebrated. What follows is a humorous example of how complicated this can be. (We received this example in our e-mail during one winter holiday season.) Jokes usually reflect some aspect of the culture that causes discomfort for people. We shared this with some human resources directors, and each said, "I wanted to laugh, but this was just too true." We think it nicely exemplifies an attempt at adapting to diversity. We invite you to reflect on and discuss how you have resolved this issue in your classroom and within your organization.

FROM: Pat Lewis, Human Resources Director
TO: Everyone
DATE: December 1
RE: Christmas Party
I'm happy to inform you that the company Christmas Party will take place on December 23, starting at noon in the banquet room at Luigi's Open Pit Barbecue. No-host bar, but plenty of eggnog! We'll have a small band playing traditional carols . . . feel free to sing along. And don't be surprised if our CEO shows up dressed as Santa Claus.

⇀

FROM: Pat Lewis, Human Resources Director
DATE: December 2
RE: Christmas Party
In no way was yesterday's memo intended to exclude our Jewish employees. We recognize that Chanukah is an important holiday that often coincides with Christmas, though unfortunately not this year. However, from now on we're calling it our "Holiday Party." The same policy applies to employees who are celebrating Kwanzaa at this time. Happy now?

⇀

FROM: Pat Lewis, Human Resources Director
DATE: December 3
RE: Holiday Party
Regarding the note I received from a member of Alcoholics Anonymous requesting a nondrinking table . . . you didn't sign your name. I'm happy to accommodate this request, but if I put a sign on a table that reads "AA Only," you wouldn't be anonymous anymore. How am I supposed to handle this? Somebody?

FROM: Pat Lewis, Human Resources Director
DATE: December 7
RE: Holiday Party
What a diverse company we are! I had no idea that December 20 begins the Muslim holy month of Ramadan that forbids eating, drinking, and sex during daylight hours. There goes the party! Seriously, we can appreciate how a luncheon this time of year does not accommodate our Muslim employees' beliefs. Perhaps Luigi's can hold off on serving your meal until the end of the party—the days are so short this time of year—or else package everything for take-home in little foil swans. Will that work? Meanwhile, I've arranged for members of Overeaters Anonymous to sit farthest from the dessert buffet, and pregnant women will get the table closest to the restrooms. Did I miss anything?

⌐

FROM: Pat Lewis, Human Resources Director
DATE: December 8
RE: Holiday Party
So December 22 marks the Winter Solstice . . . What do you expect me to do, a tap dance on your heads? Fire regulations at Luigi's prohibit the burning of sage by our "earth-based Goddess-worshipping" employees, but we'll try to accommodate your shamanic drumming circle during the band's breaks. Okay???

⌐

FROM: Pat Lewis, Human Resources Director
DATE: December 9
RE: Holiday Party
People, people, nothing sinister was intended by having our CEO dress up like Santa Claus! Even if the anagram of "Santa" does happen to be "Satan," there is no evil connotation to our own "little man in a red suit." It's a tradition, folks, like sugar shock at Halloween or family feuds over the Thanksgiving turkey or broken hearts on Valentine's Day. Could we lighten up?

FROM: Pat Lewis, Human Resources Director
DATE: December 10
RE: Holiday Party
Vegetarians!?!?!? I've had it with you people!!! We're going to keep this party at Luigi's Open Pit Barbecue, whether you like it or not, so you can sit quietly at the table farthest from the "grill of death," as you so quaintly put it, and you'll get your #$%^&*! salad bar, including hydroponic tomatoes ... but you know, they have feelings, too. Tomatoes scream when you slice them. I've heard them scream, I'm hearing them scream right now!

⟵

FROM: Teri Bishops, Acting Human Resources Director
DATE: December 14
RE: Pat Lewis and Holiday Party
I'm sure I speak for all of us in wishing Pat Lewis a speedy recovery from her stress-related illness, and I'll continue to forward your cards to her at the sanatorium. In the meantime, management has decided to cancel our Holiday Party and give everyone the afternoon of the 23rd off with full pay. Happy Chanukah-Kwanzaa-Solsti-Rama-Mas!!

What is funny to one person may be an affront to another. In the culturally proficient organization, people in Pat Lewis's position would have known the diversity of the coworkers. However, when someone errs due to ignorance, this error can be used as a teachable moment. When changing from a traditional Christmas party to a culturally proficient Winter Celebration, some people will not understand. They will say, "What difference does it make? Well why do we have to suffer because of a few of them? They don't have to come if they don't want to. Just give them the day off. This is America; they are supposed to adjust to us." In addressing these concerns, first acknowledge these feelings. People truly feel oppressed by the changes. Remind people that Christmas is a religious holiday (i.e., a "holy day") and that it is inappropriate to celebrate at work the holy day from any faith tradition. Second, take the time to gently remind people that when an organization makes a commitment to cultural proficiency, everyone changes. As you adapt to diversity, accept the creative challenge to do things differently and to do different things. A Winter Celebration party is often a good place to start.

Learning Organizations

Imagine working in a place that never learned from its mistakes and was always reinventing the proverbial wheel. This nightmarish dystopia keeps no historical records of what was done in the past and how it worked. The people from each department do not talk with people from other departments, so no one really knows what is going on at an organizational level. Consequently, resources are not shared; information is held closely until it does no one any good. There is no cross-training, and orientation rarely helps newly hired personnel to adjust to the organization's culture. This organization does not learn and is therefore not a "learning organization" (Senge, Kleiner, Roberts, Ross, & Smith, 1994; Senge et al., 1999; Wheatley, 1994).

A *learning organization* takes advantage of its successes and failures by talking about them and learning from them. No new project is begun without first seeing what can be learned and used from past activities. In this type of organization, the walls between the departments are porous: People are encouraged to talk with one another, sharing information and resources. People dissect their successes with as much curiosity as they do their failures. If you succeed only by accident, you minimize your chances of repeating your success. Here again, we see the principle of intentionality. Pay attention to what you are doing and go into each activity with the intention of being better—of being culturally proficient. After completing an activity, take the time to debrief, so that you and all who are involved can learn from the experience (Wheatley & Kellner-Rogers, 1995).

Guidelines for a Learning Conversation

At the classroom level, you can apply the idea of being a learning organization by engaging the learners in learning conversations. The guidelines for a learning conversation are few and simple (Senge et al., 1994):

- Slow down.
- Listen to understand.
- Suspend certainty.
- Encourage differences.
- Ask yourself, Why not . . . ? What if . . . ? Why now . . . ?
- Ask yourself, What does this say about me . . . ?
- Speak from your own experience.

1. *Slow down.* Take all the time you need to give your full attention to the task. If the task is to debrief an activity or to mediate a conflict, set aside the time to do it.

2. *Listen to understand.* Many of us listen to hear when the speaker breathes so that we can jump in, or we listen to hear how wrong the speaker is going to be, or we listen to see whether the speaker is going to agree with us. Many of us just look as though we are listening, when we are really just waiting to make our own points. If you listen to understand, you are assuming, as Virginia Satir (1972) says, that something about what the speaker is saying is right. You are listening to hear what it is.

3. *Suspend certainty.* Suspend the certainty that you are right. Suspend the certainty that you know everything you need to know. Suspend the certainty that the speaker is wrong—again. When you suspend certainty, your walls are less rigid and your boundaries are more flexible. You are ready to learn.

4. *Encourage differences.* In valuing diversity, you want to hear opinions that differ from yours. You encourage your learners and your colleagues to challenge you to learn and grow.

5. *Ask yourself, Why not . . . ? What if . . . ? Why now . . . ?* These questions are especially important when you hear things that you immediately disagree with.

6. *Ask yourself, What does this say about me . . . ?* Be sure to ask this question when someone has stepped on your one good nerve, when you are ready to walk away in disgust or lash out in anger.

7. *Speak from your own experience.* You have as much voice as you use. Use "I" statements. What you say will be much more powerful if you say "I" and speak about your own experience, instead of using the vague and generic "you" or the nonspecific "them."

Debriefing Questions

Guidelines for a learning conversation will help you get started and stay focused. When you are ending the conversation, it is important to take the time to assess what you did and how well you did it. The following debriefing questions may help you in that process.

- What did you notice?
- What surprised you?
- What was missing for you?
- What did you get?

- How can you use it?
- What do we as a group want to do or change?

1. *What did you notice?* The learners may not be prepared to talk about what they noticed, so you may need to repeat the question gently. What did you notice? What did you notice about yourself? What did you notice about the people in your group? What did you notice about the process? What did you notice? This question is particularly useful when you are working with people who are quick to state what was wrong and what ought to be done next. This question asks people to slow down, and it invites people to notice the subtler aspects of the situation, including the nonverbal behavior. Answers to this question often result in greater insights and learning.

2. *What surprised you?* This question (as opposed to "What did you dislike?") invites people to speak nonjudgmentally about whatever happened.

3. *What was missing for you?* This question asks people to describe what they were looking for and didn't get. It invites the learners to speak for themselves and not for anyone else. This question is particularly helpful when people in the group tend to generalize their experiences to the entire population. "What was missing for you?" refocuses them on their own experiences.

4. *What did you get?* Sometimes when the instructor asks, "What did you learn?" the learners reply, "Nothing!" This question is a bit broader and invites the learners to think broadly about their experience.

5. *How can you use it?* This question helps the learner make the transfer from the learning experience to an application in life outside the classroom.

6. *What do we as a group want to do or change?* This question implies that each individual's actions have implications for the entire group.

Activity

Try using these debriefing questions the next time you lead an activity. Notice the difference in the quality of responses and in the tone of the room by asking the softer questions that invite the learners to go deeper in their exploration of what they have learned. You may record what you notice here.

_____

_____

_____

_____

_____

_____

_____

_____

〰

Using Inclusive Language and Inclusive Materials

You may find many more new ways of engaging in the classroom as you move toward cultural proficiency. Talk with your colleagues about classroom practices that involve more people, that acknowledge invisible handicaps, and that use inclusive language. *Inclusive language* is the use of words and phrases that embrace each member of the group. No one is treated or viewed as an outsider, and no one feels like an outsider. This may mean learning to say a few phrases in the native language of your learners. Beware not to make the same mistake that the professor at the State University did in Chapter 5, when he spoke bad Spanish to Portuguese students. Talk with your learners about their learning styles, and encourage them to critically reflect on their texts.

When teaching an undergraduate class on African American women, Dr. Barbara Campbell was very excited to have found a text that approached the topic with sound research and comprehensive coverage of the material. She was quite surprised and then pleased when a student remarked, "Dr. Campbell, this isn't a book about all black American women; this is a history of middle-class black women."

Now some instructors will say, "We have no choice about textbooks. We have to teach what the district tells us. Besides, there is no culture in math." We answer by noting, "Everything is culture bound." When stuck with inadequate textbooks, you can teach your learners to examine their texts to see whose story is being told. You can also encourage them to seek supplemental materials that add to what is in the text when giving them assignments. As for math not being culture bound, include anecdotal comments about how Greeks, Romans, Arabs, Chinese, and Egyptians contributed to various mathematical processes and theories. Such comments may be just the spark a learner needs to engage with the material. Just think of the high-level thinking skills employed in such activities—analysis and synthesis that are basic to problem solving.

A very bright student we know struggled through her first year of Hebrew and passed only with the help of a generous tutor and take-home exams. Some time after that, when exploring the Kabbala, she learned that each Hebrew letter had a mystical significance. Her comment was, "If I had only known about this aspect of the language when I was studying, it would have been a lot more interesting and would have made it a lot easier for me." We thought that it would have been a lot more work, but because her interest was piqued, she would have done the extra work enthusiastically.

Learning what you can do to enhance the cultural knowledge in your classroom may take extra work on your part. We hope that your interest will be piqued as well. Just as a committed relationship requires the work of both partners, cultural proficiency requires the commitment and work of those who aspire to it. You may need to take or give special classes or workshops initially to build your skills in assessing curriculum and in acquiring the knowledge to supplement them. You may also need to set aside special times for engaging in learning conversations with your colleagues about your *praxis*, the practice of your teaching craft.

Activity

With your colleagues, reflect on the following questions: What are you doing? What are the values that inform your choices? How are people responding to your work? How are you growing and changing because of your intention to become a culturally proficient instructor?

———————————————————————————————

———————————————————————————————

———————————————————————————————

———————————————————————————————

———————————————————————————————

———————————————————————————————

———————————————————————————————

———————————————————————————————

Intentional Communities of Practice

An outgrowth of and corollary to your involvement in learning conversations with your colleagues and in your classrooms is that you will also be building your own community of practice. We belong to many communities of practice (Wenger, 1998). A *community of practice* is any group to which you belong that has specific knowledge unique to that group, a particular way of doing things, and members who are identified by behaviors reflecting this knowledge and way of doing things.

Your communities of practice may include your family, your work group, your sorority, or your church congregation. Geographical lines do not mark communities in this sense. A community of practice is a psychosocial community, bound by its group identity and its group practice. As an instructor, your place of employment may be an unintentional community of practice that you would not have chosen for yourself. You may be part of an organization that has policies and practices clustering around the points of cultural incapacity and cultural blindness on the cultural-proficiency continuum. In this case, this community of practice would be decidedly unintentional for you.

In addition to various unintentional communities of practice, you may be part of at least one *intentional community of practice*, one that you have chosen for yourself that includes a group of instructors who have made a commitment to examine their praxis. This community becomes your intentional community of practice—a community of learners. The key to intentional communities of practice is the extent to which people discuss, formally or informally, their praxis.

The other intentional community of practice to which you belong is your classroom. As you teach, you convey your values in overt and covert ways. The learners in your classroom will respond to one another within the boundaries you set and in accord with the examples of your own behavior. The classroom therefore becomes a community of practice in which you offer a silent or direct invitation to grow toward cultural proficiency along with you. In this way, you are creating a community of learners within your community of practice. Etienne Wenger (1998) admonishes us that in a community of practice, we understand that learning is a process of participation, whether for those who are new to the group or for those who have been there a long time. Culturally proficient learners understand that learning is continuous and ongoing. It is not limited to a particular classroom or to certain hours during the day.

Culturally proficient instructors place the emphasis on learning rather than on teaching by finding ways to use and develop the teachable moments that occur in the daily activities of the learners. In culturally proficient classrooms, both the instructors and the learners are engaged in designing activities that will enhance and enrich their learning experiences and their interactions with one another. Within this community of practice, the instructor will explore with the learners the interrelationship between what is going on in the classroom and what the learners do outside the classroom as they engage with other communities of practice (Wenger, 1998, p. 249).

Going Deeper

Identify some of your own communities of practice. Are you currently in a psychosocial community in which you can explore your culturally proficient praxis? Observe yourself for a few weeks, and notice how (or whether) you invite the learners in your classroom to engage in culturally proficient behavior. What aspects of your community of practice are you considering changing after reading this chapter?

_____

_____

_____

_____

_____

_____

_____

_____

_____

_____

_____

_____

_____

NOTES

Institutionalizing Cultural Knowledge

Changing for Differences

Acquiring cultural proficiency is not an event; it is a process that takes a lifetime.

People who are culturally proficient want to learn about new cultures. They want to learn how to navigate in new cultures. They solicit feedback from members of new cultures in order to improve their effectiveness in communicating and solving problems. Likewise, culturally proficient schools and other organizations highly value learning about the cultures that are present within them. Culturally proficient instructors want to learn about the various cultures represented in their classroom. They recognize that in learning about other cultures, they will continuously expand their knowledge. These instructors also know that learning about other cultures is basic to being effective instructors. As effective instructors, they directly help some learners and indirectly serve as a role model to all learners.

Getting Centered

Think of a time when you were in a setting that was totally new to you: The people were new, their interests may have been new to you, and the locale may have been new for you. Remember how you felt and how you reacted. What is it you wanted to know, either before arriving or shortly thereafter?

_____

_____

_____

_____

_____

_____

_____

⚞

Components of Institutionalizing Cultural Knowledge

The essential element *institutionalizing cultural knowledge* comprises two key components: learning about other cultures, including the culture of your own organization, and learning how other people experience those cultures. Culturally proficient organizations and instructors fully incorporate both components. Learning about other cultures goes much deeper than the typical *heroes-holidays-and-haute-cuisine* or *food-fun-and-fiesta* activities in which many organizations typically engage. Clearly, these activities may serve as an entry point for some learners or as part of a greater menu of experiences that promise ever-deeper learning. In addition to these activities, however, culturally proficient instructors want to know the history, the accomplishments, and the trials and tribulations of the people of a given culture.

For culturally proficient instructors, a culturally diverse classroom is a learning laboratory. Through meeting people from other cultures, these instructors are motivated to read, to have conversations, and to reflect on their own responses to others. Their curiosity knows no bounds. They understand that teaching learners from their own culture differs from teaching learners from cultures other than theirs. At the same time, they understand that the intercultural differences that make a difference center on worldview and values. Culturally proficient instructors examine their own biases, expectations, and views of other cultures. They know that they must be aware of any limitations they have developed so that

they can put these limitations aside when working with learners who differ from them. They also know that even when learners look like them, they cannot assume that the cultural similarities go beyond appearances.

✐

Reflection

What new cultural groups have you encountered in the recent past? How well did you know the culture? What prepared you to interact with people from the culture? What more would you like to have known? What do you still want to know about the culture?

_____

_____

_____

_____

_____

_____

_____

✐

Learning about the culture of your organization involves what Argyris (1990) describes as "double-loop learning." In *single-loop learning,* you identify a problem, identify alternative solutions, and take action. In *double-loop learning,* you become a student of your own culture, both individually and organizationally. You identify a problem, identify alternative solutions, select alternatives based on the organization's core values or beliefs, implement the solution, monitor the implementation, gather data, compare the data with the core values, modify solutions as needed, and continue the process. In essence, you not only strive for a solution, but you also want to match solutions to your core values. You develop a high value for data-driven strategies, benchmarks pegged to your core values and beliefs, and you accept no excuses for poor performance.

Sam Brewer, Rose Diaz-Harris, Charlene Brennaman, and Ed Gonzales are meeting to discuss the work of the district's technology and diversity committees. Their common concern is the equitable distribution of resources. Charlene began the conversation, "I think what we need to do is survey what hardware and software technology we currently have in the schools, find out which kids are using it, brainstorm a variety of solutions for making better use of what we have, compare those solutions with our criteria, and implement the most viable solution. Within a year or two, we should have some good results."

Rose responded, "You know, your idea is good, but I am concerned that it does not go deep enough. It seems to me that we need to know more about our current practice. For instance, I am interested to know which teachers and counselors use technology, how they use technology, what their training needs are, and how they view their students' skill levels."

With this response, Rose was taking the discussion to a deeper level. She was prompting them to think about the culture of the school as to how technology was viewed and valued and who needed what levels of training—all this before developing a plan for acquisition of hardware and software.

Sam and Ed nodded in agreement with Rose's suggestion. Ed said, "Yes, that makes sense, and it will allow us to more effectively implement the plan when we know people's needs."

Sam continued the discussion, "I can see the value of this approach. This way we will be able to determine who values the use of technology. I certainly don't want to see machines sitting unused in classrooms. It is important that we help our colleagues to see how the use of technology supports our instructional goals. Also, I would like to push our thinking. I am interested to find out the demographics of students' use of technology."

Charlene, "I am not sure I follow you."

"I think it is important to gather data on which courses are using technology and to get a profile of student use. My hunch is that students from the East Side of the community are exposed to far less use of technology in their classes. In fact, I would go so far as to guess that when they use computers, it is for drill lessons."

In gathering data on each of these concerns, the members of these committees will be getting a more complete look at the culture of their school. This is not to be constructed as a "gotcha" exercise, but as a realistic look at current practice. With these data, the educators, students, and members of the community will be able to make informed decisions about these curricular-related issues.

One sure way to gather relevant information about your organization is to ask various constituent groups about their experiences with the organization. Learning how people experience the organization does two important things. First, it provides the organization with valuable data on successes and areas of needed improvement. Second, it honors the respondents by demonstrating that they have something to teach us, too. Both the organization and the members of the new culture assume the roles of teacher and learner.

━━

Reflection

Focus on a learner in your classroom who is from a culture about which you know little. What questions do you have about how this person learns best? What do you know about this person's cultural values regarding learning? What do you know about the recent history of this learner's people? What would you like to know from this learner about her or his experiences in your classroom, in your school, or in your organization? Take a few minutes and jot down your responses or reactions to these questions. Perhaps you want to list additional questions you have.

━━

In the study of culture, the topic of organizational culture is some-times overlooked. Schein (1989) and others have helped us to see that organizations indeed have distinct cultures. Through the study of your organization, you can learn many valuable things, such as how the expressed values of the organization (e.g., a school district) may differ from the values perceived by the learners served by the organization. For example, you may see in a school's mission statement or statement of core values the words, "All children can learn." On examination of the achievement data, however, you learn that a significant portion of children are not learning. Consequently, you know there is a disconnect between what is said and what is done. Argyris (1990) describes this as the difference between espoused theory and theory in use. The conflict between espoused theory and theory in use is prevalent within schools that have significant numbers of students from low-income backgrounds or from communities of color.

Sam Brewer, speaking to members of the Diversity Committee, says, "The key words here are demographics and diversity. Take note of our reading in Reeves [2000]. Listen to these two comments that I pulled from reflection papers: 'Given the diversity of our community, these kids are doing pretty well.' 'For our demographics, I am pleased with how well our students are doing. In reality, they are getting an awful lot out of the cards they were dealt.' "

"What I see here, people," Sam says, "is what Reeves called 'code words' or using academic language as epithets. This does not reflect much cultural competence in your roles as instructors."

Reflection

Which groups of learners in your classroom are not performing as well as they should be? List the words used to describe them. How does this list compare with the sentiment in your organization's mission statement or core values? What meaning does this have for you?

Institutionalizing as a Process, Not an Event

Often, when we are teaching about cultural proficiency, some people want to be "certified" as culturally competent or proficient. That does not surprise us: Who would not want to be certified culturally proficient? As we work to become culturally proficient and struggle to institutionalize cultural knowledge, the focus must be on lifelong learning. The road to cultural proficiency is a lifelong journey because there is so much to learn. Institutionalizing the process of learning removes it from the realm of the special occasion and places it among things as basic and as important as brushing one's teeth.

When institutionalizing cultural knowledge as an instructor, you have both formal and informal learning opportunities. You can take classes and attend workshops. You can also learn about yourself, your organization, and others in less formal settings. By taking advantage of teachable moments, you will learn about and practice appropriate behaviors as you ask questions of others, respond to inquiries, and volunteer information about your culture and the culture of your school or other organization. The organization that institutionalizes cultural proficiency continuously examines its policies and practices, and it manifests in its policy and practice an in-depth understanding of the organization's culture and the culture of the individuals within it.

Going Deeper

With a small group of your colleagues, describe in detail the unwritten rules of your school or organization. What are the stated values, and what are the actualized values? How often do your core values conflict with those of your organization?

_____

_____

_____

_____

_____

_____

↠

Part III

From Reflection to Engagement

11

A Call to Action

*Once you know about cultural
proficiency, you will never be the same.
Even if you do nothing, you are acting
out of choice, not ignorance.*

You have read this book because you want to be a culturally proficient instructor. We started with an invitation, and we end with a challenge. We invited you to think, to observe, and to reflect. We now challenge you to act. You now have the tools and the knowledge to assess your own behaviors and those of your organization within the context of cultural proficiency.

In the first five chapters, you learned basic terminology, the barriers to cultural proficiency, and the cultural proficiency continuum. The next five chapters provided you with information about the essential elements of cultural proficiency. These elements are the competencies or standards by which organizations and the people in them plan for change and measure their accomplishments. When integrated into organizational policies and individual values, the essential elements become the standard practice, rather than isolated events or individual behaviors. People and their organizations become culturally proficient when specific strategies and behaviors are practiced consistently.

As we have walked with other instructors on the road to cultural proficiency, we have noticed that they predictably move through five levels of preparation: awareness, assimilation, processing, development, and deconstruction. If you have read this far, you have completed the first level. You are aware. You have become a student of your own reaction to people, organizations, and the issues that arise from diversity. Your reactions are clues to continued, deeper learning.

Many people assume that cultural proficiency is a process for learning about others. By now, you know that cultural proficiency involves primarily learning about yourself and your organization. That is why we call it an inside-out approach to diversity. It starts with the self. At the same time, even as you read this book, you acquired additional facts and information that will help you in understanding the differences between yourself and others. This learning must continue. As a culturally proficient instructor, you will seek out information about the people you teach. You will integrate into your subject matter materials information about the history, culture, and sociohistorical context of the people you work with.

One of the hardest tasks to complete as you move toward cultural proficiency is the processing of your own issues regarding power and oppression. As you completed the activities in this book and spent time with the reflection questions, you were also processing your feelings, acknowledging your biases and prejudices, and drawing new conclusions about who you are and who you can be. As an instructor, it is important to remember that oppression and power imbalances create obstacles for some people that do not exist for others. Developing the capacity to confront your own issues with power and oppression enables you to recognize these issues and neutralize them in your classroom.

In addition to whatever training you received to be an instructor, you need specific skills and techniques to manage the dynamics of difference and to facilitate effective cross-cultural communication in your classroom. Some very important steps include developing facilitation skills to foster healthy communication, to encourage critical reflection by your learners, and to engage with the learners as a community of practice. You can do this by watching others who are skilled, by taking workshops on advanced facilitation skills, and by practicing.

As you continue to reflect on your teaching practices—realizing that what was effective with one group of learners may not be successful with others—you are going to decide to stop doing some things and to change others. This process is called "deconstruction and reconstruction." You want to *deconstruct*, assessing and examining what you do, and then you want to *reconstruct*, reordering or restructuring your craft of teaching practices. When you experience frustration and failure, having the capacity to check yourself and your delivery systems for what did not work and being receptive to learning different strategies shows that you are a reflective practitioner of your craft.

In planning your content and delivery systems, several considerations will improve your effectiveness in a diverse classroom. You may want to consider some of these approaches as you work on your craft:

- Team teach so that you can have a mentor or be a mentor.
- Establish a process for sharing activities and incidents throughout the course of instruction. The classroom experience is most vivid when learners can relate in-classroom learning to their lives outside the classroom and when you can critically reflect on what they do with others outside the classroom.
- Engage in strategic systematic coaching with your colleagues.
- Hold a retreat for yourself and other instructors to deal with *your and their* issues of oppression and power so that you and they are more comfortable and better prepared to facilitate classroom discussions.
- Obtain instruction on how to infuse issues of diversity into your classes, and how to respond to learner statements of bias and injustice. You do not have to have all the answers, but you must be comfortable fielding the questions.
- Learn not to be afraid to recognize your mistakes. Acknowledge them, learn from them, and redirect them to more effective actions.
- Develop a process for mentoring, coaching, and collecting ideas. One of the most invaluable resources for instructors is the successful experience of colleagues.

⟵

Reflection

What will be your next steps?

_____

_____

_____

_____

_____

_____

⟵

⟿

Activity

At the outset of this book, you compiled a list of teaching practices you considered particularly effective. Pull out that list again, and add any items you now feel should be added. With a group of your colleagues, analyze the relationship between your list of teaching practices and the essential elements of cultural proficiency.

_____

_____

_____

_____

_____

_____

_____

_____

⟿

What Difference Do You Make Together in Your Community of Practice?

By completing the preceding activity, you have gained immediate evidence that a community of practice is useful and makes a difference. Moreover, if you are committed to becoming a culturally proficient instructor, you probably have already begun to think of the people with whom you can work to make a difference. In your community of practice, you will learn and grow together as you create nurturing, supportive, growth-producing environments for the learners in your classroom.

⟻

Reflection

What difference do you make with others in your community of practice?

_____

_____

_____

_____

_____

_____

_____

⟻

D
r. Barbara Campbell had been asked to address the newest group that had completed the Leadership Maple View program. She had talked with them about her favorite topic, cultural proficiency, and was reassuring them that they could indeed make a difference.

"Each of us has one little pebble of influence," she said. "Now you can take that pebble and stick it in your pocket or drop it into your purse, and you are right—nothing will change. You could also take your one little pebble and drop it into the river. You may see a splash; it might hit a little fish on the head. But again, you won't see much change.

"Another option for you is to join with the others here who also have pebbles, and together, you can make some strategic decisions. You could, for example, band together and decide that the river is not the best place for pebbles. For instance, at the lake, if you dropped all your pebbles into the same spot at the same time, you could make quite a splash.

"Friends, as leaders of this city, you have already banded together, and the city of Maple View is the kind of pond where you can make a difference. Let us all pledge here tonight to drop our pebbles of cultural proficiency into our Maple View pond. Each of us—at the schools, at the hospital, downtown, East Side, and West Side—together, we will make a big difference."

Going Deeper

What will you do with your pebble of influence?

_____

_____

_____

_____

_____

_____

_____

_____

_____

_____

_____

_____

_____

References

Andrews, William L., & Gates Jr., Henry Louis (1999). *The civitas anthology of African American slave narratives*. Washington, DC: Counterpoint.

Argyris, Chris. (1990). *Overcoming organizational defenses*. Boston: Allyn & Bacon.

Ball, Edward. (1998). *Slaves in the family*. New York: Ballantine.

Banks, James A. (1999). *An introduction to multicultural education*. Needham Heights, MA: Allyn & Bacon.

Boyer, Mark; Ellis, Kaethe; Harris, Dolores R.; & Soukhanov, Anne H. (Eds.). (1983). *The American heritage dictionary* (2nd college ed.). New York: Dell.

Carmichael, Stokely, & Hamilton, Charles. (1967). *Black power: The politics of liberation in America*. New York: Random House.

Cross, Terry; Bazron, Barbara J.; Dennis, Karl W.; & Isaacs, Mareasa R. (1993). *Toward a culturally competent system of care* (Vol. 2). Washington, DC: Georgetown University Child Development Program, Child and Adolescent Service System Program.

Darling-Hammond, Linda, & Ball, Deborah Loewenberg. (1997). *Teaching for high standards: What policymakers need to know and be able to do*. Retrieved April 10, 2001 from the World Wide Web: www.negp.gov/Reports/highstds.htm

Franklin, John Hope, & Moss, Alfred A., Jr. (1988). *From slavery to freedom: A history of Negro Americans* (6th ed.). New York: McGraw-Hill.

Freire, Paulo. (1987/1999). *Pedagogy of the oppressed*. New York: Continuum.

Gordon, Milton M. (1978). *Human nature, class, and ethnicity*. New York: Oxford University Press.

Haycock, Kati. (1998). Good teaching matters: How well-qualified teachers can close the gap. *Thinking K-16, A Publication of the Education Trust, 3*(2), 1-16.

Hernandez, Hilda. (1999). *Teaching in multicultural classrooms*. Englewood Cliffs, NJ: Prentice Hall.

Kent, Karen. (1999). Teachers developing as professionals. In *California field guide for teachers' professional development: Designs for learning*. Sacramento: California Department of Education.

Lindsey, Delores B. (1999). *Evidence of engagement: A study of CSLA's ventures leadership training program participants' engagement of teachers in creating an environ-*

ment for powerful learning [CD-ROM]. Abstract from: ProQuest File: Dissertation Abstracts Item: 9956040.

Lindsey, Delores B. (2000, September). *Spotlight on teaching.* Paper presented at the Orange Unified School District Staff Development Day, Orange, CA.

Lindsey, Randall B., Nuri Robins, Kikanza, & Terrell, Raymond D. (1999). *Cultural proficiency: A manual for school leaders.* Thousand Oaks, CA: Corwin.

Loewen, James W. (1995). *Lies my teacher told me: Everything your American history textbook got wrong.* New York: New Press.

McAllister, Gretchen, & Jordan Irvine, Jacqueline. (2000). Cross cultural competency and multicultural teacher education. *Review of Educational Research, 70*(1), 3-24.

Myrdal, Gunnar. (1944). *An American dilemma* (Vol. 11). New York: Pantheon.

Noguera, Pedro. (1999). *Equity in education: What difference can teachers make?* Sacramento: California State Department of Education, California Professional Development Consortia.

Ogbu, John. (1978). *Minority education and caste: The American system in cross-cultural perspective.* New York: Academic Press.

Palmer, Parker J. (1998). *The courage to teach: Exploring the inner landscape of a teacher's life.* San Francisco: Jossey-Bass.

Reeves, Douglas B. (2000). *Accountability in action: A blueprint for learning organizations.* Denver, CO: Center for Performance Assessment.

Riehl, Carolyn J. (2000). The principal's role in creating inclusive schools for diverse students: A review of normative, empirical, and critical literature on the practice of educational administration. *Review of Educational Research, 70*(1), 55-81.

Rosenholtz, Susan J. (1991). Shared school goals. In *Teachers' workplace* (Vol. 12). New York: Teachers College Press.

Satir, Virginia. (1972). *People making.* Palo Alto, CA: Science & Behavior Books.

Schein, Edgar. (1989). *Organizational culture and leadership: A dynamic view.* San Francisco: Jossey-Bass.

Senge, Peter; Kleiner, Art; Roberts, Charlotte; Ross, Richard B.; & Smith, Bryan S. (1994). *The fifth discipline fieldbook: Strategies and tools for building a learning organization.* New York: Doubleday.

Senge, Peter; Kleiner, Art; Roberts, Charlotte; Roth, George; Ross, Richard B.; & Smith, Bryan S. (1999). *The dance of change.* New York: Doubleday.

Sergiovanni, Thomas J. (1994). *Building community in schools.* San Francisco: Jossey-Bass.

Singham, Mano. (1998). The canary in the mine. *Phi Delta Kappan, 80*(1), 9-15.

Takaki, Ronald. (1993). *A different mirror: A history of multicultural America.* Boston: Little, Brown.

Thomas, Kenneth, & Kilman, Ralph H. (1974). *Conflict mode instrument.* Sterling Forest, Tuxedo, NY: Xicom.

Ury, William. (1991). *Getting past no: Negotiating with difficult people.* New York: Bantam.

Vigil, James Diego. (1980). *From Indians to Chicanos: A sociocultural history.* St. Louis, MO: Mosby.

Wenger, Etienne. (1998). *Communities of practice: Learning, meaning and identity.* New York: Cambridge University Press.

Wheatley, Margaret J. (1994). *Leadership and the new science.* San Francisco: Berrett-Koehler.

Wheatley, Margaret J., & Kellner-Rogers, Myron (Technical Advisers), Jordan, Peter J. (Executive Producer). (1995). *Lessons from the new workplace* [Video]. (Available from CRM Films, 2215 Faraday Avenue, Carlsbad, CA 92008)

Further Reading

In addition to the references cited in the text, we recommend these additional resources to aid you in developing your own cultural proficiency as an instructor.

Berliner, David C., & Biddle, B. J. (1996). *The manufactured crisis: Myths, fraud, and the attack on America's public schools.* Reading, MA: Addison-Wesley.

Bracey, Gerald. (2000). The 10th Bracey report on the condition of public education. *Phi Delta Kappan, 82*(2), 133-144.

Coleman, James S.; Campbell, E. O.; Hobson, C. J.; McPartland, J.; Mood, A.; Weinfeld, F.; & York, R. L. (1966). *Equality of educational opportunity.* Washington, DC: Government Printing Office.

Delpit, Lisa. (1995). *Other people's children: Cultural conflict in the classroom.* New York: New Press.

Freire, Paulo. (1998). *Pedagogy of freedom: Ethics, democracy, and civic courage.* New York: Rowman & Littlefield.

Hall, Edward T. (1959). *The silent language.* New York: Doubleday.

Karns, Michelle. (1998). *Ethnic barriers and biases: How to become an agent for change.* Sebastopol, CA: National Training Associates.

Kellner-Rogers, Myron. (1996). *A simpler way.* San Francisco: Barrett-Koehler.

McIntyre, Alice M. (1997). *Making meaning of whiteness: Exploring racial identity with white teachers.* Albany: State University of New York Press.

Murray, Carolyn B., & Fairchild, Halford H. (1989). Models of black adolescent academic underachievement. In Reginald L. Jones (Ed.), *Black adolescents.* Berkeley, CA: Cobb & Henry.

Naisbitt, John, & Aburdene, Patricia. (1990). *Megatrends 2000: Ten new trends for the 1990s.* New York: William Morrow.

Nieto, Sonia. (1999). *Affirming diversity: The sociopolitical context of multicultural education.* New York: Longman.

Owens, Robert G. (1995). *Organizational behavior in education.* Boston: Allyn & Bacon.

Sleeter, Christine E., & Grant, Carl A. (1994). *Making choices for multicultural education: Five approaches to race.* New York: Merrill.

Wartell, Michael A., & Huelskamp, Robert M. (1991, July 18). *Testimony of Michael A. Wartell & Robert M. Huelskamp, Sandia National Laboratories, before Subcommittee on Elementary, Secondary, and Vocational Education, Committee on Education and Labor, U.S. House of Representatives.* Washington, DC: Government Printing Office.

Index

**CORWIN
PRESS**

The Corwin Press logo—a raven striding across an open book—represents the happy union of courage and learning. We are a professional-level publisher of books and journals for K-12 educators, and we are committed to creating and providing resources that embody these qualities. Corwin's motto is "Success for All Learners."